D0818665

Career Planning and Management
A Managerial Summary

Elmer H. Burack
Professor of Management
University of Illinois Chicago

This book draws importantly on the concepts
and approaches found in Elmer H. Burack and
Nicholas J. Mathys, *Career Management in
Organizations: A Practical Human Resource
Planning Approach.* Brace-Park Press, 1980.

Published 1983
by Brace-Park Press
P.O. Box 526
Lake Forest, IL 60045

Library of Congress Cataloging in Publication Data

Burack, Elmer H.
    Career Planning and Management

    Includes bibliographical references.

ISBN-0-942560-07-8

Composed By: **NORSHORE**
              Northbrook, Illinois 60062

Dedicated with love and affection to
my family. Their loyalty, support
and understanding made this book
possible.

To Ruth, Chuck, Bob, Alan and Shana.

Elmer H. Burack

June 1983

This book draws importantly on the concepts and approaches found in:

Human Resource Planning: A Pragmatic Approach to Manpower Planning and Development. Elmer H. Burack and Nicholas J. Mathys. Brace-Park, 1980.

ACKNOWLEDGEMENTS

The writer is pleased to acknowledge the numerous and useful comments regarding earlier drafts of this book. Many helpful ideas were received from:

Maryann Albrecht, Ph.D., College of Business Administration; University of Illinois, Chicago.

Donald D. Baker, Director, Career and Human Resource Development, Rochester Institute of Technology.

Linda Anne Blatt, Instructor, Iowa State University; Consultant, Sheldon Associates.

Ralph Catalanello, Ph.D., School of Business, Northern Illinois University.

Robert E. Edwards, Vice President, Personnel; Southeastern Life Insurance Company.

Richard B. Frantzreb, Editor and Publisher; Advanced Personnel Systems.

John A. Hooper, Manpower Planner, Tektronics, Inc.

Donald R. Marshall, Corporate Director, Labor Relations & Personnel Planning; Bell & Howell.

Nicholas J. Mathys, Ph.D., College of Business; DePaul University.

Sheldon Pinsky, Ph.D., Iowa State University; Director, Sheldon Associates.

Phyllis Sandell, Director of Management Development, Evangelical Hospital Association.

Edward Yost, Instructor: Ohio State University.

Also, Sherry Stansbury, Editor provided helpful

ACKNOWLEDGEMENTS

editorial assistance and **Alan J. Burack,** University of Illinois, provided helpful work in copy editing.

Although pleased to acknowledge the assistance of these people, as author I must assume responsibility for the final product -- this I do.

Elmer H. Burack

CONTENTS

EXHIBITS

EXHIBITS

This managerial summary presents an overview of the what, why, and how of career management in organizations (CMO). There is information about the conceptual framework of CMO; what it is designed to do; what to look for in developing programs; the objectives and obstacles that can be expected; and the ultimate advantages resulting from the program. Rather than a "how-to" book for the practitioner, this summary offers an introduction to this exciting new field. As such, it should appeal to a wide range of people in business, industry, and education.

Specifically, for line managers and officers, this summary provides a necessary data base for their level of involvement in career matters. They will be able to talk knowledgeably with people in charge of human resource programs. Similarly, reading these resource notes will enable presidents and chief executive officers to determine better the quality of leadership in this area.

For personnel officers, this book provides an understanding of work done by career specialists and shows how to relate this work to conventional personnel functions. Personnel staff can in turn approach their own jobs better equipped for implementing such career programs as skill development, designing career ladders, and individual assessment. Even experienced practitioners have found this type of overview helpful in assuring perspective on their specialized areas.

Students will find this a compact resource book directing attention to key elements of CMO. Professors can use it as a handy supplement for courses on personnel, organization, and management in MBA programs.

Included here are various case studies showing how career planning has been successfully integrated in selected companies. There are also specific forms for discussing managerial attitudes towards career issues, assessing individual needs, establishing knowledge levels for analysis, career pathing, individual development, auditing career planning systems, and more. A

==

bibliography of materials relating to CMO is located at the end of this summary.

These resource notes roughly follow the chapter format and topic development of **Career Management in Organizations: A Practical Human Resource Planning Approach** by Elmer H. Burack and Nicholas J. Mathys (Lake Forest, IL: Brace-Park Press, 1980). Some charts and forms are also reprinted from this edition. For a more extensive investigation of CMO, we suggest referring to the larger, more detailed text.

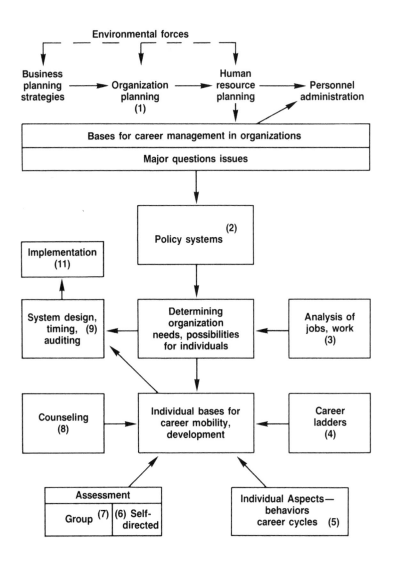

Environmental forces

Business planning strategies → Organization planning (1) → Human resource planning → Personnel administration

Bases for career management in organizations

Major questions issues

Policy systems (2)

Implementation (11)

System design, timing, auditing (9)

Determining organization needs, possibilities for individuals

Analysis of jobs, work (3)

Counseling (8)

Individual bases for career mobility, development

Career ladders (4)

Assessment

Group (7) | (6) Self-directed

Individual Aspects— behaviors career cycles (5)

Introduction

Perspective

INTRODUCTION

PERSPECTIVE

CAREER MANAGEMENT SYSTEMS AND HUMAN RESOURCE PLANNING

Career management in organizations (CMO) is a system designed to meet individual career needs -- for job advancement, extension of skills, or the enhancement of human experience on the job -- and to relate these needs to the future requirements of the organization. As such, activities of CMO involve a range of career matters relating to individuals within the context of human resource planning (HRP).

But before we begin a discussion of CMO, a model can provide a ready frame of reference. Each chapter of this book opens with a diagram outlining the organizational functions of CMO. In addition, the area being discussed in each chapter is shaded in the diagram for easy reference. The item numbers correspond to chapter numbers.

A Framework for Understanding Career Management

As you can see from the model, career activities in organizations are wide in scope. CAREER MANAGEMENT arises from the twin demands of the external environment and the internal organization of the enterprise. From the environment come factors such as economic opportunity, competitive threats, and legal actions to which policy makers and other officials must respond. To deal with these external forces an enterprise determines business strategies in such areas as marketing and finance, and carries out the ORGANIZATION PLANNING (1) to help accomplish these. The latter creates or modifies positions and authority structures of an organization and so affects staffing and future skill needs. The

3

==

translation of organization planning into personnel requirements, time schedules, and skill needs is the goal of human resource planning (HRP): that is, having the right numbers of people at the right place at the right time, who have the appropriate skills. Career management exists to develop programs that match the skills of individual employees with the demands of HR staffing and timing.

The items below refer to those on the chapter diagram and deal directly with the activities of CMO.

* **Career policy/systems (2):** Career management policies clarify the organization's commitment to job opportunities. A policy statement usually indicates exactly how the organization will support careers by outlining structure and procedure.

* **Analyses of jobs/needs (3):** Analyses of jobs and work needs of the individual provide information about skills and abilities required for training and development.

* **Career ladders (4):** Career ladders point out logical channels between positions for transfer and promotion, and in turn define the ways in which skills are best developed.

Career pathing, a program design of work and training for an individual, involves employees in a series of inter-related considerations and activities, among them:

* **Career attitudes/behavior (5):** Personal considerations in career management are motivation, goals, values, and where a person is in a career life cycle.

* **Self-directed assessment (6):** A self-directed analysis of personal goals, values, interests, and work style helps an individual take charge of a career -- and is basic to individual career planning.

* Group assessment (7): This is an official
  assessment of potential provided by information
  from supervisors, personnel specialists,
  performance tests, and past work experience.

* Counseling (8): Job counseling provides a
  sounding board for individual ideas, assists in
  dealing with career problems, checks the
  feasibility of career plans, and directs a
  person to other sources of information.
  Information from employees about their career
  goals is combined with information from the
  organization concerning job requirements and
  career ladders. Career planners then organize
  this data into a workable system.

* System design (9): A CMO system design
  determines the main functional activities of
  CMO, establishes workable linkages for these and
  then sets timetables for these to occur.
  Continuing change and new organizational needs
  require periodic audit to ensure needed
  adjustments or corrections.

* Major questions (11): Career-related questions
  continually arise in the planning for and
  conduct of career programs. Officials, line
  managers, and staff groups will all be involved
  at various times in the organization and
  administration of career activities.

The Complex of Activities in CMO

As the diagram illustrates, career management is an
integral part of a system that encompasses organization
planning, personnel function, and individual needs.
Although it is useful to identify each area of activity,
the model of CMO tends to simplify the interconnectedness
and overlapping of functions in an enterprise. In
reality, an enterprise is much more complex.
    For instance, business strategy establishes the
nature of markets, services, and products offered by the

enterprise.   This overall planning sets into motion
internal organizational changes as firms expand, contract,
change directions, up-date work systems, respond to new
legislation, or cope with competitive tactics.
Organization planning in turn must establish the core of
work functions, employee relationships, and skills to
carry out these overall enterprise plans.   Human resource
planning serves to translate enterprise plans into general
staffing needs and also to bring about adjustments in
enterprise plans that appear unworkable.   Career
management is the central programming activity of human
resource planning.   Plans for officer succession,
management development or ensuring equal employment
opportunities, for example, fall under its jurisdiction.

One example of the intricacies of the system is
management development.   Traditionally an important
consideration in organization planning, management
development ensures continuity of the organization and
renewal of people indispensable to a firm's success.   But
to maintain this foundation of managerial expertise, an
organization must reckon with the personal wants and needs
of the individual manager.   In this way, management
development is both a core activity of HRP as well as an
important function of CMO.

STRUCTURE OF CAREER FUNCTION

Many organization activities are currently career
related.   But they are often placed in different areas to
benefit specialized interests or economic action.   For
example, people who compile job analyses may report to a
wage and salary unit or an engineering unit in operations.
Line managers often perform important career functions and
are crucial to the success of a program.   As part of the
annual personnel review, they gather information on work
performance or assessment of potential that is important
for needs analysis in career planning.   Most job
counseling occurs as regular communication between line
managers and their unit members.   Moreover, in order to
construct career ladders CMO relies on the experience of
line managers and personnel officers as well as on data
from job analyses and compensation specialists.

==

For these reasons, the primary functions of CMO are
directing action research, planning career-related
procedures, coordinating activities among departments, and
then administering programs. Depending on economic size,
market served, and organization goals, these
responsibilities can require a single person or small
group to carry them out. Since job counseling has grown
in importance recently and often requires professional
training, some firms may hire a specialist. Small firms
that cannot afford to maintain a regular CMO staff may
simply expand the responsibilities of personnel managers
and staff. Outside consultants have been used often in
counseling on the design of the installation. Because of
their related functions, CMO and HRP may be combined in
some firms and assigned to one person or a personnel
planning unit.

In any case, close relationship with, as well as
coordination among, business and organization planners,
human resource planners, personnel officers, and line
managers is essential.

CURRENT ISSUES AND CHALLENGES

A successful career management system can propel both
the individual and the organization toward a future where
work performance is mutually beneficial. Current research
indicates, however, that effective career management is
becoming increasingly complicated and at the same time
more important in organizations. Some companies that
don't have CMO systems need them; those that have
initiated CMO programs in the past need to revitalize them
to meet the rapid changes affecting business and society
today.

Issues Affecting CMO

At present, organizations and individuals face a time
of turbulence and change. Organizations are beset with
increased competition from foreign companies, changing
technology, inflation, high interest rates, and operating
complexities. Government regulations have been changing

traditional practices of hiring, training, promotion, and compensation. In addition, changes in the work ethic have taken place within the last ten years as a new generation moved into the organizational structure. Organization members are currently better educated, more concerned with personal well-being in careers as well as in life, and more amenable to organizational approaches to individual development than they were in the past.

Individuals have high career expectations, yet they are currently faced with increased competition for jobs, and reduced job opportunities. Thus, at a time when greater emphasis is placed on the value of a career and its personal meaning, job security and a sense of career possibility for the individual may be undermined.

Specific developments that are causing growing concern among career planners are as follows.

* Turnover rates now average 30, 40 and even 50 percent across many occupational positions in organizations. They are particularly high in sales and clerical positions, but turnover is not confined to these areas.

* Layoffs and unemployment, related to changes in technology, the economy, and shifts in consumer needs, have created unstable working conditions for individuals as well as an unstable internal labor market for organizations.

* Growing numbers of job or promotion transfers are rejected if they require a geographical move. A recent issue of THE CONFERENCE BOARD reports a rejection rate of one out of four offers among employees in large corporations.

* Programs designed to assist women, minorities, and the handicapped have not significantly altered the composition of the occupational structure. Although women are entering the labor force in great numbers, most are entering occupations traditional for women. Ten percent or less of low-level managerial positions are now held by women. Furthermore, women as a

==

group have made little progress in receiving
equal pay for equal work, although this is
starting to change in large corporations.

*   Succession into upper levels of management is
       becoming increasingly competitive as the
       demography of the organization reflects the
       "baby boom" generation.

These current developments raise disturbing
questions. Can individuals achieve a meaningful career in
the rapidly changing organizations that characterize
modern society? Can organizations adapt sufficiently and
survive at a time when many workers demand challenge and
growth in their work? These questions point to the need
for ongoing career development to link individual need
over time with the changing goals of organizations.
Career management approaches are as important in periods
of great company growth as in periods of no growth or even
decline in sales.

Career Terminology: Human Experience and No Room at the
Top

A major factor contributing to the emergence of
career management in the first place and to its growing
complexity now is the new meaning attached to the word
CAREER. Traditionally, a career meant being promoted up,
or to a new job or a different occupation. However,
modern study indicates that much individual fulfillment on
the job comes not exclusively from the hope of moving up,
but from the work itself, how individuals feel about
themselves, and whether they are achieving some of their
life goals.

This new value of career as human experience also
relates to new facts of organization life, which are
sometimes denied or ignored. For instance, with the
influx of the "baby-boom" generation into middle
management plus the extension of the retirement age, there
are a limited number of positions in upper levels of the
managerial pyramid. Yet organizational pressures to move
up are still reinforced by existing systems of reward and

punishment. Some people who refused promotions in the past have often been ignored when other opportunities (e.g., lateral transfers) arose. Policy makers in general have been reluctant to accept the fact that some people are content to do a job well and have their weekends free instead of being promoted to more responsibility.

CMO needs to incorporate the new realities of organizational life and individual values into programs that address both. There has always been a different focus for each of the two aspects of career management: ORGANIZATION PLANNING places priority on future staffing needs, cost-effective performance, and flexible plans to cope with change; INDIVIDUAL CAREER PLANNING centers on personal values, life goals, and even a change in employers. The present potential for widening these differences can be averted by consistent efforts to identify common objectives and then by moving in the same direction.

Challenges for the '80s

Career management has suffered in the past from a lack of monitoring, coordination, and integration within organizations. Many programs have been undertaken in a piecemeal way that ignores long-range planning and development. Career management systems in the 1980's will have to meet the following challenges.

*   Reflect both short- and long-term business needs.

*   Guide, direct, and transfer individuals into promising job possibilities and even different fields if necessary.

*   Create systems that more fully integrate the career activities of personnel specialists with individual planning and counseling functions.

*   Strengthen the primary position of line management in its ability to function well within career systems.

===

* Maintain a stable career program in a time of rapid change.

* Build new career management systems on a foundation of basic personnel and management activities such as job analysis and thoughtful compensation programs.

* Audit, maintain, and introduce necessary changes into the career management system to assure its vitality.

* Develop more flexible and responsive ways of processing information and individual skills, aptitudes, and location preferences as well as available jobs.

Thoughtful planning and programming of career activities is justified as economically sound, as good management practice, and as a direct way of improving employee involvement in organization interests. A growing number of firms are starting to hang numbers on the benefits and costs of career management systems in organizations. Study results are starting to be reported in the literature. These studies are not without difficulty but initial returns look quite promising. Contained in the following chapters are ways of insuring such careful attention to career management.

APPENDIX

Discussion Questions and Issues

1.   Based on the general systems model for a career system, what problems will likely be encountered in attempting to coordinate and integrate career planning activities with those of human resource and business planning?

2.   Referring again to the general systems model, what are the likely consequences of deficiencies in such areas as (a) career ladder construction, and (b) counseling?

3.   What new challenges and problems are likely in a career planning approach to areas such as management development?

4.   What new(er) career issues do you anticipate in the next year or two? What is likely to be organizations' responses to these?

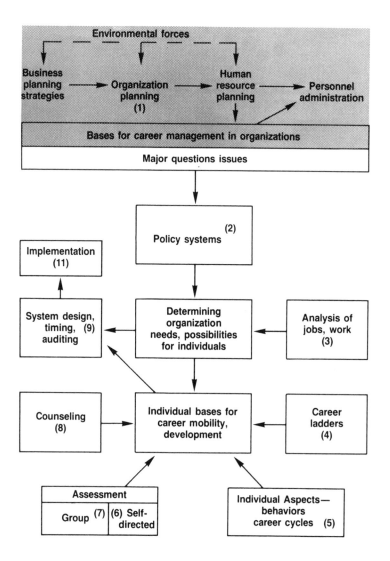

Chapter One

Career Planning: An Overview

CHAPTER ONE

INTRODUCTION

ORIGINS OF CAREER PLANNING

New Concepts of Careers

Motivational models

Dual labor markets

New Techniques: Work Analysis and Individual
Evaluation

CAREER ISSUES: ORGANIZATIONAL POLICY AND INDIVIDUAL
ATTITUDES

The Attitude Form

Uses for the Attitude Form

Exhibit 1-1: Factors and Trends Furthering Career
Thinking

Exhibit 1-2: Managerial Attitudes on Career Issues

APPENDIX

Discussion Questions and Issues

CAREER PLANNING: AN OVERVIEW

INTRODUCTION

In addition to the income from products and services and the costs of furnishing them, personnel practices and the quality of individual relationships within an organization also influence costs. An individual's satisfaction or dissatisfaction on the job is reflected in terms of turnover, absenteeism, tardiness, willingness to extend oneself, cooperation, and even creativity. Career planning in an organization can improve the outlook, expectations, and realization of its members. And by improving human experience on the job, an effective career program can in turn strengthen organizational efficiency.

There are four elements to effective career planning within a career management framework; the individual, the work, the organization, and future developments. The individual is the vortex around whom revolve the issues of work, the organization, and the patterns of change. However, concern for individual career development is placed within a context of organizational possibilities.

As a result of this concentric relationship, CAREER PATHS exist on two levels:

*   to connect the individual's work with his or her life situation, and

*   to connect today's individual with tomorrow's organization needs.

These two interpretations of career paths -- one favoring the individual, the other favoring the organization -- need not be incompatible. Indeed, it is the role of career management in organizations to establish a common ground between them.

==

One way of understanding how to establish this common ground is to look at how an individual interprets future organizational requirements. Too often in the past, much planning for the individual has been "numbers planning" -- seeing the individual as a commodity to fill a certain position in the organization. But a person's sense of career possibilities depends on how carefully job requirements in terms of specific skills and abilities are communicated by the organization. An individual can interpret these organizational requirements alternately as opportunities, threats or business as usual. This in turn affects the clarity of personal career paths and, more generally, career planning.

Major changes in the educational system have contributed to the emergence of career concepts. Educational delivery has diversified with programs ranging from preparation of specific skills (e.g., computer programming) to career-oriented university degrees (e.g., in advertising and business as well as law and medicine). These changes in formal education are paralleled by introduction of informal and continuing education programs. In addition, due to rapid social and technological changes, many adults now consider learning an on-going process. Such LIFE-LONG LEARNING, supported by universities, professional societies, and community groups, has become a commitment to the work lives of a growing number of people.

SELF-DIRECTED LEARNING is a response to the notion of taking charge of one's career. Such learning is tailored to professional needs and human development. However, although exposed to a new era of learning concepts, some people are not quite knowledgeable enough to activate fully personal learning mechanisms. This possible deficiency should be considered in organizational career plans.

SELF-ASSESSMENT of one's career is based on self-directed learning and career inquiry. As a method, self-assessment utilizes a set of tools and procedures to help the individual think through his or her goals, values, career interests, and work skills. Self-assessment is a process of self-diagnosis in addition to the services traditionally offered by professional counselors.

==

Motivational models. In considering CP we need to be
aware of the behavioral ideas about why and how people do
things. Several models of motivation that explain career
behavior are detailed in Chapter 5. A brief summary
follows here.

*   Needs theory, developed first by psychologist
     Abraham Maslow, posits a hierarchy of personal
     needs. Once the basics of food, clothing,
     shelter, and economic security are attained,
     individuals seek to satisfy a higher order of
     needs, such as social relationships, recognition
     of others, and personal achievement.
     Satisfaction of these higher order needs is
     increasingly being sought in the work place.

*   Path-goal is a newer motivational theory. It
     emphasizes specific goal-directed behavior in
     pursuit of personal goals and career objectives.
     This theory has major implications for CP in
     that it focuses an individual's attitude on
     particular preferences and emphasizes (career)
     goal-directed behavior.

*   Exchange between employer and employee is
     another behavior theory gaining favor in
     organizations. The opportunity to satisfy goals
     is recognized by both parties to be a
     cooperative, mutually beneficial effort.

Dual labor markets. New thinking about careers also
takes into consideration the existence of dual labor
markets. The number, type, and availability of external
sources of labor affect internal personnel planning and
procedures. Career planning is an end product of overall
HUMAN RESOURCE PLANNING (HRP), or manpower planning. HRP
calculations provide the basis for recruiting from
internal and external labor markets and in this way
establish the standards for career planning. In turn,
these staffing calculations must be closely tied to the
general plans of the organization.

==

New Techniques: Work Analysis and Individual Evaluation

    A second development that has encouraged career
planning is the availability of techniques for qualitative
and quantitative evaluation of systems of jobs or types of
work.

*   Occupational analysis provided by the U.S.
     Department of Labor is one example of these new
     methods. Occupational analysis focuses on three
     areas: (1) the development of accurate
     descriptions of job attributes and personal
     skills; (2) the grouping of common job features
     into occupational "families" that contain
     different job titles; and (3) the identification
     of skills that bridge occupational families and
     facilitate mobility between jobs.

*   Needs analysis takes into account the current
     state of individual skills and the desired state
     of individual performance in the future. This is
     a diagnostic technique used to prescribe the
     skill and abilities a person should acquire for
     a targeted job.

*   Performance appraisal falls somewhere between
     traditional judgment based on past performance
     and assessment of future potential. As such, it
     emphasizes human development.

*   Assessment of potential tries to predict the
     future performance possibilities of an
     individual. Newer approaches often use group
     techniques to gather data systematically.
     Information is then used for personnel
     selection, hiring, and promotion, as well as for
     feedback to participants to further self-
     development.

*   Job analysis as a traditional method is
     currently undergoing substantial changes.
     Individual jobs are now viewed as part of work
     systems so that communications and cooperative

===

work relationships take on more importance.
More rigorous techniques and even self-analysis
instruments are increasing the usefulness of
data derived from these approaches. Job
descriptions that result from job analyses are
more frequently being developed in terms of the
specific behaviors needed for success on the
job.

*   Psychological instruments -- e.g., the Kuder,
     Strong, Wonderlic, and Minnesota tests -- have
     been used for some time to identify individual
     preferences, interests, aptitudes, and values.
     However, these have been greatly supplemented by
     newer instrumentation that deals with aspects of
     leadership, achievement motivation, and career-
     life stages. The results of these tests
     frequently require interpretation from trained
     personnel people, professional counselors, or
     vocational psychologists. Such information is
     important to individual career planning and has
     been increasingly used in management development
     and succession planning analyses.

*   The federal government has also contributed many
     models and instruments for organization and
     systems analysis and measuring individual
     aptitude and potential. For example, the U.S.
     Air Force carried out much of the initial work
     on manpower forecasting models.

Support for CP

     Other factors accounting for the emergence of career
planning are the recent changes in society, government,
organizations, and individual needs. Within each of these
areas, there is a set of distinct factors and trends that
furthers career thinking (see Exhibit 1-1). Noteworthy is
the relatively recent prominence of career matters since
about 1975 compared to largely macro-type manpower
planning which began in the mid 1960's.

EXHIBIT 1-1:   Representative Factors and Trends Furthering Career Thinking

Social

- changing character of work ethic
- increased longevity
- shifts in proportion of age groups
- increased level of education
- new female independence
- increase in number of women working
- increase in number of minorities in universities and work place

Governmental

- equal employment legislation
- affirmative action programs
- legislation regarding age discrimination and extending retirement age
- increased government employment
- government actions (e.g., career techniques and personnel research) serving as models for private enterprise

Organizational

- development of the computer
- need for better assurance of human resource planning in relation to business planning
- availability of improved personnel instruments
- desire to improve employee satisfaction
- desire to improve interviewing, assessment, and promotion
- search for productivity improvement in light of the peaking of technology

Individual

- emphasis on higher order needs
- increased desire to achieve independence and influence work variables affecting self
- multiple careers
- dual-career thinking (people and companies)
- complexities of job planning for the future

SOURCE: Adapted from Elmer H. Burack and Nicholas J. Mathys, Career Management in Organizations: A Practical Human Resource Planning Approach (Lake Forest, IL: Brace Park Press, 1980), p. 14.

==

CAREER ISSUES: ORGANIZATIONAL POLICY AND INDIVIDUAL
ATTITUDES

Many of the philosophical ideas and specific
approaches to CP run counter to established organizational
procedures, policies, and practices. Thus, in attempting
to implement a career program, a manager must be prepared
to deal with a number of career-related issues. Many
supervisors, managers, and policy officials may hold
outmoded or prejudiced attitudes regarding an employee's
age, sex, race, and the capabilities related to these.
Some may assume, for example, that performance decreases
with age or that women cannot do "such and such" type of
work. In addition, some line managers may be unwilling to
take responsibility in human development, erroneously
thinking that individuals can and should independently
pursue their careers without organization support.

The Attitude Form

We have developed an attitude form to help reveal
important career issues (see Exhibit 1-2). This same form
has also been used to provide useful information for
workshop discussions involving all levels of company
managers and officials. For organization officials, line
managers, and career specialists there are eight basic
career-related issues that can be assessed using the
attitude form. These issues are as follows.

*   Organizational responsibility in career planning
      (questions 1, 2, 3, 4, 9, 14, 16, 17): Such
      responsibilities are based increasingly on legal
      requirements as well as employee expectations.

*   Individual responsibility in career planning
      (questions 3, 11): Active participation in
      planning one's own career is not only self-
      satisfying but often the only practical basis
      for progress.

*   Role of line managers and personnel in CP
      (questions 5, 6, 9, 15, 17): Line managers are

EXHIBIT 1-2: Managerial Attitudes on Career Issues

1. I believe the company has an obligation to provide a
    lifetime career plan for every employee.   A   SA   NS   SD   D

2. One should have made a career choice by the time one
    is 30 years old.   A   SA   NS   SD   D

3. One can change to a better job after the age of 50.   A   SA   NS   SD   D

4. It is difficult to satisfy young college graduates
    because they want to get ahead fast.   A   SA   NS   SD   D

5. Women cannot be advanced in a corporation.   A   SA   NS   SD   D

6. I should be able to guide my subordinates and make
    work suggestions to them.   A   SA   NS   SD   D

7. I should appraise each employee about possible career
    paths and requirements for them.   A   SA   NS   SD   D

8. Employees need not inform me of their career
    aspirations.   A   SA   NS   SD   D

9. Promotion and transfers should be strictly according
    to set rules.   A   SA   NS   SD   D

10. If an employee is very good at his or her present
    assignment, I may not recommend him or her for a
    promotion since replacement is difficult.   A   SA   NS   SD   D

11. I am responsible for the career choices of my
    subordinates.   A   SA   NS   SD   D

12. I don't have anything to do with the promotion
    system. It is the personnel department's job.   A   SA   NS   SD   D

13. I should tell my subordinates about chances in other
    departments, other branches, divisions, etc., where
    their qualifications and experiences will help them.   A   SA   NS   SD   D

14. I should assist my subordinates in their growth by
    sending them to training programs, company classes,
    continuing education, etc.   A   SA   NS   SD   D

15. I should inform my manager about promising employees
    so that he or she can observe them.   A   SA   NS   SD   D

EXHIBIT 1-2: Managerial Attitudes on Career Issues (cont'd)

16. It is the company's responsibility to apprise each of its employees about organization career paths and requirements.   A SA NS SD D

17. The personnel needs of the organization should override the personnel needs of units or departments.   A SA NS SD D

18. It is the organization's responsibility to apprise members about opportunities in various departments, divisions, etc.   A SA NS SD D

19. Organizations should actively assist individuals' growth by sending them to training programs, continuing education activities, etc.   A SA NS SD D

20. Job posting represents an effective way to carry out an equal opportunity policy for "internal" job recruiting.   A SA NS SD D

21. Widely available information for organization members is needed on wage levels and pay guides in order to develop an effective career program.   A SA NS SD D

22. Women as females are intimidated by virtue of their sex in matters of appraisal, promotion, and/or their work-related activities by male organization members.   A SA NS SD D

23. Women supervisors tend to be tougher with female subordinates than in their relationships with male subordinates.   A SA NS SD D

24. Women tend to be less aggressive than men when it comes to upward career mobility and are more prone to "let things work out by themselves."   A SA NS SD D

Key: A = Agree SA = Slightly agree NS = Not sure SD = Slightly disagree
      D = Disagree

SOURCE: Reprinted from Elmer H. Burack and Nicholas J. Mathys, Career Management in Organizations: A Practical Human Resource Planning Approach (Lake Forest, IL: Brace Park Press, 1980), pp. 20-21. May be used for internal organization purposes without permission. Commercial application requires the expressed consent of the publisher and author.

central figures in providing information and assessments for general human resource planning and in employee counseling. The personnel department provides support for the manager-employee relationship, monitors activities, and assumes the lead in general employee planning.

*   Role of line managers in promotion opportunity and decisions (questions 5, 6, 7, 8, 9, 10, 11, 12, 13, 14): This role is critical. If the supervisor blocks a promotion because he feels a person is "indispensable" to his or her own operation, then the long-term interests of the individual and the organization may be defeated.

*   Promotion opportunities for women and minorities (questions 9, 12, 11, 23, 24): Such opportunities will only be accomplished when a determined effort is made at all organizational levels.

*   Activities in support of individual development and careers (questions, 14, 18, 19, 21): These should be tied concretely to both organization needs and employees' career ambitions.

*   Job or career opportunity and communication (questions 16, 20, 21): Two different levels of communication exist in the organization; (1) the organization needs information to meet operational requirements and legal demands, and (2) individuals need information to make sound career decisions.

*   Organization of the CP effort (questions 9, 12): This effort is dependent on many variables. Whether the function is taken over by an existing personnel unit, a new one is created for this purpose, or line management absorbs many of these responsibilities, it should be uppermost in the minds of those in charge that personnel backs line management. The relationship of line managers to their workers

==

must be preserved.

Uses for the Attitude Form

The information provided by a career attitude
instrument can be used in several ways. One way is simply
to summarize the responses, identifying those issues that
have high degrees of agreement or disagreement among
organization members. The areas of high disagreement
would be key issues to focus on before proceeding with
implementation of CP. Another way to use the form is to
consider what is possible in an organization or what
accomplishments have actually been made in career-related
activities. Thus, it is necessary to balance the
difference between individual opinion and company
practice, with what has been successful in other
organizations and the reasons underlying these successes.
To this end, a manager must have information about
alternative systems as well as the history of the
enterprise.

APPENDIX

Discussion Questions and Issues

1. Consider your organization or one you are familiar
    with. What are some of the underlying assumptions of
    line managers and officials regarding systems and
    people that would likely have a negative effect on
    introducing or extending HR planning?

2. With changes in the legislation affecting mandatory
    retirement, now age 70 rather than 65 for most firms,
    what new(er) HRP's might be indicated?

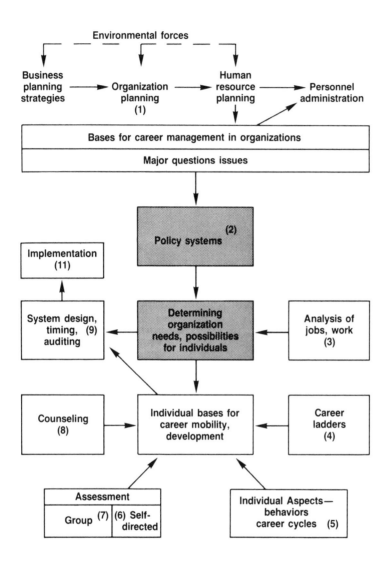

Environmental forces

Business planning strategies → Organization planning (1) → Human resource planning → Personnel administration

Bases for career management in organizations

Major questions issues

Policy systems (2)

Implementation (11)

System design, timing, auditing (9) ← Determining organization needs, possibilities for individuals ← Analysis of jobs, work (3)

Counseling (8) → Individual bases for career mobility, development ← Career ladders (4)

Assessment
Group (7) | (6) Self-directed

Individual Aspects— behaviors career cycles (5)

Chapter Two

Career Policy, Systems, and Approaches

CHAPTER TWO

INFLUENCES ON CAREER PLANNING

    Legal Considerations

    Public Initiatives

    Management Philosophy

    Other Factors Affecting CP

ORGANIZATION FRAMEWORK FOR CAREER MANAGEMENT

    Activities of CP

        Job/work analysis

        Basic personnel practices

        Action research

    Career Management "line" Functions

    Definitions of Careers

    CMO Systems Components

        Stage 1, formulative

        Stage 2, emergence

        Stage 3, contemporary

        Stage 4, the leading edge

    Auditing the Activities of CMO

MODEL STRUCTURE OF A CAREER POLICY PROGRAM

Exhibit 2-1: General Audit - Career Management System

Exhibit 2-2: Structure of a Career Advisory Program

APPENDIX

Discussion Questions and Issues

CAREER POLICY, SYSTEMS, AND APPROACHES

INFLUENCES ON CAREER PLANNING

Because career planning evolves gradually within an organization, a cross-section of various organizations reveals different degrees of career management policies and systems. In addition, several factors affect the degree of organizational involvement in career matters.

Legal Considerations

Equal employment legislation and affirmative action guidelines have established a basic level of organizational involvement in career management. The requirements regularly to report employment statistics in categories of race, sex, and occupational class have encouraged private enterprise voluntarily to institute nondiscriminatory practices. Moreover, the threat of individual or class action suits has further induced organizations to develop fair and equal career programs. Nevertheless, compliance with government policy has been generally slow and sporadic in the private sector. However, even with some relaxation in the enforcement or auditing for compliance with equal employment and related matters, a model of employee relationships and approaches has been established that will likely have enduring effects.

Executive Order 11246 -- Equal Employment Opportunity and Revised Orders No. 14 and No. 4 for affirmative action provides a format for human resource planning and career development. These orders detail work force analysis, individual skill development, training of supervisors in career matters, and strengthening of the personnel effort. Complete statements of these orders can be obtained from

===

the Office of Federal Contract Compliance or the Commerce
Clearing House. Highlights of the legislation are
included in the Appendix to Chapter 2 of **Career Management
in Organizations** by Elmer Burack and Nicholas Mathys.

Public Initiatives

Governmental programs for CP often establish ways to
improve personnel actions and so provide models for the
private sector. Some of these models include (1) the
executive development programs of the U.S. Department of
Agriculture, (2) personnel activities of the U.S. Civil
Service Commission, (3) programs at major military
installations (e.g., the naval unit at China Lake,
Calif.), and (4) the career program for government
employees in the Commonwealth of Pennsylvania.

Management Philosophy

A third factor affecting organizational involvement
in CP is the philosophy of the organization's leaders.
Although there is a rough correlation between
organizational size and interest in career matters (e.g.,
IBM and Control Data), managerial philosophy seems to be
of greater consequence, especially where companies have
implemented more than a minimal career program. Related
to this is the degree to which managers become actively
involved in career planning. Managerial support, coupled
with the availability of technical know-how from internal
or external sources, results in a higher degree of
commitment to the CP program.

Other Factors Affecting CP

The character of the organization itself, company
visibility, and work force composition can also determine
an organization's commitment to career planning.
Companies that have high exposure to the public and large
numbers of white collar workers -- e.g., banks, insurance
companies, airlines, financial institutions, public

==

accounting firms -- have been leaders in career
development. Among these organizations, there is a high
educational level in the work force, greater pressure to
hire women and minorities, and more opportunities for
promotion to higher managerial positions. Industrial
organizations are also beginning to improve the quality of
work life, as unions start making this a major bargaining
point. The automotive industry in the U.S. and Europe
(especially Volvo in Sweden), and U.S. companies such as
Donnelly Mirrors, Mead Paper, and some General Foods
plants, have experimented with such changes in the work
place, with varying degrees of success.

ORGANIZATIONAL FRAMEWORK FOR CAREER MANAGEMENT

The overall features of a career management system
are shaped by the main policies, people, and systems of
the organization. Policy is not a public relations effort
nor is it a bland, uniformly applicable instrument. It
must be built around the needs of a given situation.
Managerial values regarding CP form a basic part of the
organization's career environment. The concepts of career
management systems emphasizes the relationship of
individual career activities to the broader planning of
the organization. In this way, individuals facilitate
institutional plans and institutions support individual
development.

Activities of CP

Activities for career planning vary widely. Below
are some essential functions for CMO.

Job/work analysis. A CP program cannot even begin
without accurate information about jobs. A thorough work
analysis provides descriptions of each job and specifies
the amount of responsibility and work demands that a
particular job offers. Work analyses also identify
sequences of jobs that build particular skills and
"families" of jobs requiring similar skills. In addition,
because of rapidly changing environmental trends and

==

strategic activities, work analyses must be adjusted and updated continually. Further discussion of work analyses occurs in the next chapter.

   Basic personnel practices. Often neglected are personnel practices at the time of recruitment. The shaping of an individual's outlook starts at the initial job interview before hiring. Failure to communicate an accurate picture of an organization's possibilities and limitations can adversely affect an individual's motivation as well as his or her sense of promotion opportunities, work alternatives, and job satisfaction.
   These same techniques apply in orientation, training, and performance appraisals. This interrelatedness between career systems and other organizational systems emphasizes coordination, control in the sense of advisory responsibilities and administration.

   Action research. This research is focused directly on specific improvements in system performance and productivity. In terms of CP, action research analyzes ways to improve such procedures as job assessment, career development patterns, promotion, new employee expectations, effective training of supervisors as trainers, job design, and improved means of assessing potential.

Career Management "Line" Functions

   Career line functions are detailed in subsequent chapters. In general, though, line activities serve to integrate individual career plans with organizational career management. Managers need a knowledge of people -- their abilities, needs, and desires for the future. This knowledge of people is then combined with information about an organization's system and skill needs. CAREER PATHING results from this process: a design to match individual training with future work responsibilities and assignments. MANAGERIAL COUNSELING not only provides specific information about organizational needs and the means for capitalizing on them, but also helps people check the reality of their career assumptions.

==

Definitions of Careers

Career planning so far in this summary has been discussed in terms of employee expectations, skill development, and opportunities for advancement. But career thinking also takes into account the character of work in the present as well as in the future. Thus, career management includes improvement of the human experience within a particular job or a change in job, work rules or even occupation.

The increase in multiple careers in recent years provides a good example of the need for thinking broadly about individual careers. Because of demographic and economic changes, many people have had to choose a new occupation that is significantly different from what they were originally trained for. Thus, it is not unusual to see an engineer become a sales representative or an elementary school teacher become an editor of computer instruction manuals. These lateral changes between occupations, or between jobs in one company, need to be considered in career management. Also, much more attention is being given to job and occupational change strategies to maintain the interest and performance of more mature or "older" employees.

CMO Systems Components

Career management does not suddenly appear in an organization as a complete activity. The individual components evolve over time. This evolution can be traced through four distinct stages.

Stage 1, formative. This stage is characterized by informality based on tradition. Companies at this point are usually concerned with maintaining traditional career patterns and organizational relationships, while attempting to respond to specific short-run needs.

Stage 2, emergence. CMO activities emerge as organizations grow in size and face a more complicated environment. Growth leads to a need to ensure the development of key people for critical positions.

Informality gives way to formality, as basic career
information becomes available.

     Stage 3, contemporary. The contemporary career
management system is characterized by the following
features.

* job/work analysis   * career ladders

* flexibility in   * job availability
  transfer and promotion   information

* succession planning   * counseling

* formal policy   * personnel development

* employee information files   * career information

                                 * retirement planning

     Stage 4, the leading edge. By this stage,
organizations have formalized policies and procedures of
career management. Key features include comprehensive job
analysis techniques; establishment of career networks;
formalized development programs for employees; and
strategic human resource planning that seeks to link
together business and personnel planning and action
programming -- and develops the appropriate strategies for
these.

Auditing the Activities of CMO

     A critical set of activities -- fifteen methods and
practices -- is detailed below. One can rate one's
organization on each of these activities to assess the
effectiveness of the organization's career management.
     A score of 12 to 13 on "yes" indicates a rather
complete system. A score of 7 to 9 on "no" usually
indicates a system that is getting underway. However,
some enterprises that scored well on this self-analysis
form omitted critical activities such as numbers 1, 3, or
5.

===

Exhibit 2-1: General Audit -- Career Management System

	YES	EMERGING	NO

1. Policy statements that reflect
    the needs of both the organization
    and the individual.   ___   ___   ___

2. An equal opportunity system,
    facilitating an open internal
    labor market. One technique
    is job posting. It is certainly
    not free of problems, and various
    other approaches may be used or
    combined with it. Implicit in
    any approach is the intent of
    the organization; is an open
    and equal opportunity system
    really desired?   ___   ___   ___

3. Top management support,
    including budget is interpreted
    by managers to mean that "if some
    budget is provided, it must be
    important." This simply
    acknowledges an organizational
    fact of life; that these systems
    involve costs which must be
    provided for separately rather
    than coming out of operating
    budgets.   ___   ___   ___

4. Active management facilitation
    to smooth the way when problems
    have to be overcome.   ___   ___   ___

5. Integration with human resource
    and business planning systems.
    This ensures that career activities
    will be tied to organization
    realities.   ___   ___   ___

==

	YES	EMERGING	NO

6. Management accountability for
    career activities that are
    incorporated into their
    own reward system (e.g., in
    their performance appraisal)
    that prevents it from
    being just "business as usual."   —   —   —

7. Effective bases to judge
    individual abilities that
    establish successful
    placements and help reduce
    charges of favoritism.   —   —   —

8. Provisions for the
    alignment and continuing
    adjustment of organizational
    and individual needs.
    This supports the realization
    that in an environment of change
    both organization and
    individual needs are likely to
    change too.   —   —   —

9. An orientation toward people,
    not numbers. This requires
    flexibility that shows individuals
    that they do matter.   —   —   —

10. A workable communication and
    feedback system as the basis
    for career planning and
    counseling activities.   —   —   —

11. Innovative personnel
    approaches that assist self-
    renewal and ward off
    obsolescence.   —   —   —

                                          YES   EMERGING   NO

12. Action research capability
    for analyzing and evaluating
    performance and past events
    as a basis for initiating
    changes and providing guides
    for further actions.   —   —   —

13. Evaluation of system
    performance that realistically
    attempts to assess costs and
    benefits.   —   —   —

14. Acceptance of the idea that
    career decisions are mostly
    personal decisions and
    action plans, thus individuals
    take charge of their own
    careers.   —   —   —

15. Recognition that personal
    career decisions can benefit
    both organization and
    individual, so that
    institutional support is
    rational and needed.   —   —   —

                                          —   —   —
                                          YES   EMERGING   NO

MODEL STRUCTURE OF A CAREER POLICY PROGRAM

To illustrate this discussion of career matters, we have developed a structural model of a corporation's career program. This model is based on a medium-sized, vertically integrated steel company organized along divisional lines. Actually, a CMO system originates from an organization's CAREER POLICY AND MISSION STATEMENT that outlines specific goals, structure, and procedures. (For the complete career policy statement related to this model, please refer to Exhibits 2-4 to 2-6 in Burack and Mathys, Career Management in Organizations.)

The internal career system of this model organization is administered through a committee structure. Principal composition of the committees appears in Exhibit 2-2. Reponsibilities are described as follows:

* The Steering Committee provides program suggestions, progress reports, and occasionally assessments of current efforts. The fact that elected employee representatives assume action roles in its activities helps to assure the interest and involvement of organization members.

* The Organization Development Committee is the central functional unit of this network. It assesses recommendations from the Steering Committee, proposes strategies and procedures, and implements approved programs. It is the auditing coordination center and communications hub for the entire career program.

* The Management Training and Development Committee convenes at its own discretion and represents the real (political) power in the organization. It reviews and considers feasibility of proposals and programs. This committee provides an important monitoring and assures active involvement of senior managers, thus gaining their support as well as that of their units.

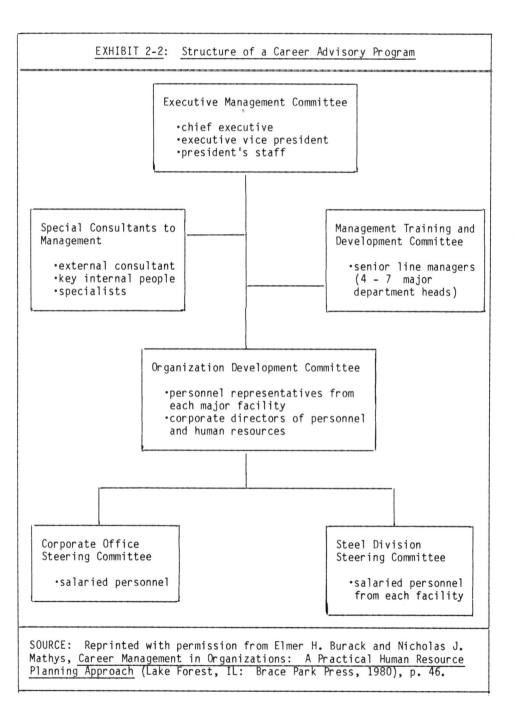

EXHIBIT 2-2: Structure of a Career Advisory Program

Executive Management Committee

- chief executive
- executive vice president
- president's staff

Special Consultants to Management

- external consultant
- key internal people
- specialists

Management Training and Development Committee

- senior line managers (4 - 7 major department heads)

Organization Development Committee

- personnel representatives from each major facility
- corporate directors of personnel and human resources

Corporate Office Steering Committee

- salaried personnel

Steel Division Steering Committee

- salaried personnel from each facility

SOURCE: Reprinted with permission from Elmer H. Burack and Nicholas J. Mathys, Career Management in Organizations: A Practical Human Resource Planning Approach (Lake Forest, IL: Brace Park Press, 1980), p. 46.

==

* Special Consultants serve top management by assisting in program design.

* The Executive Management Committee provides the functions of review, audit, and budget approval. The fact that it authorizes necessary funds, executive actions, and personnel to initiate, maintain, and expand the program assures a career planning activity that is seen as meaningful in the organization.

In addition to this organization structure, an effective career policy also outlines an individual's responsibility to assess personal career ambitions and initiate actions that prepare for career mobility and promotion.

Aside from this general committee structure for CP, career programming usually involves some reorganization of the PERSONNEL UNIT. For the company model illustrated, activities related to CP at the divisional level were wholly incorporated within the general activities of division personnel managers and their training and development staff. At the headquarters level several important changes were made in the PERSONNEL FUNCTION. First, a position of supervisor of human resource planning was established to work in connection with business planning in order to accomplish overall staffing analysis and needs. Second, a position for supervisor of career planning was established to carry out the planning for a start-up program, oversee supervisory orientation and training for new roles, and to coordinate the internal system once it was underway.

==

APPENDIX

Discussion Questions and Issues

1. Quality of work life and job enrichment have received much press. What projects might be considered for action research?

2. A medium-sized bank was considering an HRP program but hadn't "as yet" fully accomplished a general planning effort. Comment.

3. A large hospital has launched a well publicized HRP program, primarily for succession planning and management development. The program covers 10 percent of the employees. Comment.

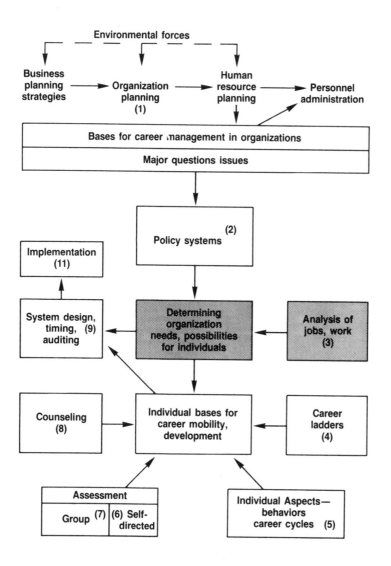

Environmental forces

Business planning strategies → Organization planning (1) → Human resource planning → Personnel administration

Bases for career management in organizations

Major questions issues

Policy systems (2)

Implementation (11)

System design, timing, auditing (9)

Determining organization needs, possibilities for individuals

Analysis of jobs, work (3)

Counseling (8) → Individual bases for career mobility, development ← Career ladders (4)

Assessment

Group (7) | (6) Self-directed

Individual Aspects— behaviors career cycles (5)

Chapter Three

Analyses of Jobs and Individual Work Needs

CHAPTER THREE

BASIC APPROACHES IN ANALYSES OF JOBS AND INDIVIDUAL NEEDS

    Work Analysis and CMO

        Job data base

        End behaviors

    Ways to Improve Work Analysis

    Needs Analysis

    Behaviorally Anchored Work Statements and Needs Assessments

    Needs Analysis and CMO

DEVELOPMENTS IN JOB INFORMATION

    Building the Information Base

    Accuracy and Application

Exhibit 3-1: Comparison of Job Descriptions at Williams Hospital

Exhibit 3-2: Individual Needs Assessment Analysis

APPENDIX

    Discussion Questions and Issues

CHAPTER 3

ANALYSES OF JOBS AND INDIVIDUAL WORK NEEDS

BASIC APPROACHES IN ANALYSES OF JOBS AND INDIVIDUAL NEEDS

Virtually all career management functions depend on accurate information on jobs and work structures. Unfortunately, traditional job analyses are often too narrowly focused or outdated to be of much service to today's increasingly complex career planning. Clearly a revitalization of the concept and the practice is needed. We have used the term WORK ANALYSIS here to indicate a more comprehensive and timely approach to the methods of job analysis.

Fundamentally, work analysis defines job requirements in terms of responsibility, skills needed, and behaviors expected on the job for successful performance. Such analysis probes jobs as they currently exist and as they are likely to be altered by future staffing needs and methods changes.

Work analysis and NEEDS ANALYSIS are closely related, and both are essential for CMO. Work analyses identify specific work behaviors -- i.e., physical skills, mental abilities, general and technical knowledge, past work experience -- that are necessary for successful job performance. Needs analysis tries to match organization needs with individual needs. In this way, a person's skills and knowledge are systematically compared to job requirements. Needs analysis helps direct career pathing for the person by specifying an individual's work experience, training, and education. These career paths can then prepare people to meet requirements for future jobs as well as current reassignment, job changes or promotions.

Work Analysis and CMO

Work analysis is important to career management for several reasons:

1. Individual career planning requires a working knowledge of jobs being considered.

2. Such job information is used in personnel development, performance appraisal, assessment of potential, and succession planning.

3. It is the central basis of job evaluation for wages and salaries.

4. It is linked to traditional personnel functions like recruitment, counseling, and training.

To be useful, work analysis must identify both job dimensions and the individual skill and abilities needed to fulfill them. In addition, work analysis must be timely to be relevant. For example, a great deal of the information used today violates the spirit and letter of equal employment opportunity and affirmative action guidelines. Job analysis documents will have to be updated or replaced altogether in the future.

Job data base. Every organization has formal and informal information on jobs. But sufficient information must exist to provide a reasonably accurate picture of what the job entails and to determine individual development needs. At best organizations have only an adequate base of information.

If complete overhaul of a job information system is impractical, it is better to identify priorities and work on improving targeted areas. Priorities are logically suggested by such imperatives as staffing shortages in certain departments and affirmative action pressures for promotion from low-skill jobs. For example, a shortage of management trainees might lead to studying the targeted management, stepping stones, or developmental positions. Similarly, a need to improve mobility from low-skill jobs would suggest a close examination of entry-level as well

==

as low-skill positions.

   To improve the job data base some organizations identify a common set of factors linking related work categories and then fill in the specific behaviors for a given job.

   End Behaviors. For the company, the job represents a set of responsibilities and behaviors that when successfully accomplished meets a valued objective. Thus, the focus on end behaviors is a way of measuring whether the individual effort on the job accomplished the intended objective. The kind of documentation necessary for this analysis comes from three sources:

   *   **job descriptions** outlining job responsibility
        and relationships.

   *   **job specifications** (or job specs) interpreting
        job responsibilities in terms of desired
        skills, education and training, and

   *   **work procedures** that diagrams the sequence of
        activities, techniques, and branching of a job.

Ways to Improve Work Analysis

   Job descriptions commonly use vague or abstract words such as plan, organize, direct, coordinate, control, and administer. But these general descriptions do not tell a job holder (exactly) what to do or what the ultimate objective is. How does one go about accomplishing the end behavior of "planning" or "coordinating?" In some cases, these job descriptions are cursory, thereby compounding the problem of interpretation.
   However, with some effort and concentration on specific behaviors, JOB DESCRIPTIONS can be not only updated but considerably improved. Exhibit 3-1 shows a section from an old job description at Williams Hospital contrasted with a section from the updated one. Notice how the job description was modernized to include more detail on RN work requirements and responsibilities. (The full text of both job descriptions appears as Exhibits 3-1

EXHIBIT 3-1:   Comparison of Job Descriptions at Williams Hospital

Original Job Description

TITLE: Registered Nurse

DEPARTMENT: Nursing

JOB DUTIES

1. Supervises patient care activities in accordance with the nursing care plan.
2. Uses the nursing care plan to determine patient treatment.
3. Assigns nursing care activities to team members.
4. Promotes and maintains high standards of nursing care.
5. Cooperates with other hospital personnel for the well-being of the patient.

Updated Job Description

RESPONSIBILITIES AND AUTHORITIES

A. The RN utilizes the "nursing process" for assessment, planning care, implementing plans, evaluating patient responses to the medical plan, nursing
   interventions, and revising plans as indicated.

B. Work performed:

   1. Assesses the needs and problems of patients as required.
   2. Plans for individual nursing care of each patient assigned to his or her
      team. In doing so he or she
      a. Establishes short- and long-range goals
      b. As directed by medical staff and nursing supervisor, develops and
         maintains current nursing care plans utilizing
         1) Medical care plan and orders
         2) Admission interviews and questionnaires
         3) Nursing care conferences
         4) Patient and family
         5) Allied health professionals.
   3. Utilizes the nursing care plan to qualify patient care. In doing so he
      or she
      a. Conducts conferences with team members to discuss
         1) Nursing needs of patients
         2) Priorities of nursing care
         3) Implementation of medical care plan and orders.
      b. Assigns specific nursing care activities to team members based upon
         their ability, experience, and job descriptions.
      c. Promotes the maintenance of high standards of nursing care.
         1) Performs nursing techniques for comfort and well-being of the
            patient
         2) Utilizes opportunities for teaching to improve performance and
            to enhance growth and job satisfaction of team members
         3) Assists team members with unusual and complex nursing care
            situations

   4) Adapts nursing care activities to meet the changing needs of patients and assists team members to make adaptations as necessary

   5) Cooperates with coordinator or assistant director in revision of assignments.

  d. Assures economical and safe utilization of equipment and supplies by following established procedures.

  e. Carries out physicians' orders and medical care plan accurately.

  f. Assists in diagnostic and therapeutic measures as needed.

  g. Maintains effective channels of communications.

   1) Prepares meaningful clinical records of nursing care, on a regular basis

   2) Participates in team conferences as required

   3) Keeps physician, team coordinator, and team members informed of any significant change in status of patient immediately

   4) Maintains harmonious relationships with patients, families, visitors, and staff members

   5) Coordinates nursing care activities with services provided by the "logistics" department and others to

    a) Maintain a safe, clean environment

    b) Account for all drugs, supplies, and equipment used

    c) Admit, discharge, and transfer patients in a courteous manner, following sound medical practices

    d) Provide clarification of physicians' orders relating to laboratory tests, x-rays, medications, etc.

   6) Coordinates with other departments to ensure the

    a) Upholding of hospital policies

    b) Safety of patients.

  h. Cooperates with faculties and students of affiliated educational nursing programs to achieve objectives of clinical experience as needed.

  i. Contributes to improvement of health care by

   1) Utilizing opportunities for patient and family teaching

   2) Recognizing the implication of social and economic factors upon patient's welfare and making referrals to hospital social services when needed to assist the patient and family with problems

   3) Encouraging utilization of community resources for continuity of patient care.

4. Evaluates the effectiveness of nursing care on a continuous basis:

  a. Utilizes the nursing care plan to evaluate the quality of nursing care given

  b. Participates in audit-related activities with internal and external groups as requested

  c. Cooperates in the evaluation of services provided by other hospital departments and nursing care-related committees as requested.

SOURCE: Adapted from Elmer H. Burack and Nicholas J. Mathys, Career Management in Organizations: A Practical Human Resource Planning Approach (Lake Forest, IL: Brace Park Press, 1980), pp. 74-77.

and 3-2 in Burack and Mathys, Career Management in Organizations).

Improving work analysis does not end with the job description. The next stop in an updated program for Williams Hospital was a preparation of JOB SPECIFICATIONS to determine the specific skills for satisfactory performance to facilitate training. Then a more extensive analysis of WORK PROCEDURES identified critical job dimensions of nursing so as to set up a systematic means of appraising performance.

Needs Analysis

It is important to remember that needs analysis serves both individual and organizational career planning. For the individual, counseling by a person's immediate supervisor and personnel counselors, if necessary, accompanies these procedures. For the organization, needs analysis considers current and future staffing needs, opportunities, and alternatives. When needs analysis is carried out as a career management activity, usually a specific job is targeted. When it is self-oriented, an individual usually considers several job alternatives.

The following procedures for needs analysis consider both organizational requirements and individual career plans.

1.   Determine the abilities and end behaviors of the targeted job.

2.   Secure data on employee background and review for accuracy and completeness.

3.   Compile needs analysis information that jointly views the individual and the targeted job.

4.   Formally review individual career interest and need with line managers, career counselors, and other specialists.

5.   Reconcile employee career plans, needs, and job requirements with those of CMO.

===

6. Develop individual training and educational
    programs according to a specific timetable.

7. Specify career paths.

8. Provide feedback and review.

Behaviorally Anchored Work Statements and Needs Assessments

Increasingly, job descriptions are needed that
reflect what people actually do on the job. In
particular, work analysis that tries to meet equal
employment opportunity standards usually establishes
behaviorally anchored job information. Improvements in
the RN job description in Exhibit 3-1 illustrate such
behaviorally anchored work statements. Similarly, the
amount of responsibility expected on the job needs to be
defined in terms of specific levels of authority and
division of duties. For example, say a Sales supervisor
is responsible for "identifying needs for sales programs,"
while the Assistant Sales Manager actually "contracts with
suppliers in order to secure sales." This division of
responsibilities is important, and its inclusion in the
responsibility statement of a job description or job
specification can increase the precision of needs
analysis.

A part of needs analysis involves assessing
individual abilities in terms of specific skills required
by a job. INDIVIDUAL NEEDS ASSESSMENTS, sometimes called
ABILITY ASSESSMENT SCHEMES, evaluate the relative
importance of each ability to job success. These
assessment schemes vary among organizations; some are
included in job descriptions while others find their way
to performance appraisal forms. In any case, all ability
assessments must indicate specific behaviors and
particular standards used to measure ability. As an
example, we'll use the Sales Supervisor mentioned above.
Exhibit 3-2 outlines (in simplified form) an ability
assessment of John Louis Worth.

Notice that Worth's planning responsibilities are
expressed in behavioral terms. The abilities needed for

EXHIBIT 3-2: Individual Needs Assessment Analysis

INDIVIDUAL: John Louis Worth   ACTIVITY: Planning

CURRENT POSITION: Sales Supervisor, Zone A

ABILITIES REQUIRED** IN AREAS OF PLANNING RESPONSIBILITY	ASSESSMENT OF INDIVIDUAL ABILITY*				
	Doesn't apply	Low	Some ability	Good***	Expert
1. "Assists manager in setting yearly sales objectives."					
• knowledge of market research concepts				X	
• knowledge of accounts					X
• knowledge of salespeople		X			
2. "Contracts with suppliers to secure sales and promotion incentives."					
• ability to prepare quotas			X		
• knowledge of financial features of contracts		X			
3. "Assists manager in planning yearly sales programs."					
• work with variety of staff people, salespeople				X	
• knowledge of sales budget procedure				X	

  *Assessment definitions:
        Low = needs regular assistance of supervisor or co-worker.
  Some ability = needs occasional assistance of supervisor or co-worker.
        Good = able to do most work independently.
      Expert = works independently, at times consults for other people.

 **Representative items--many more are in actual analysis.
***Target competency.

SOURCE: Based on Elmer H. Burack and Robert D. Smith, Personnel Management: A Human Resource Systems Approach (New York, NY: John Wiley & Sons, 1982), p. 486.

these planning activities are then assessed relative to
job requirements. The targeted level of competency in
this case is "good," meaning the person is "able to do
most work independently." All other levels are ranged
according to this standard.

The skills assessment or rating depends on the
assigned job responsibilities. For instance, look at item
2, "contracts with suppliers to secure sales and promotion
incentives." Mr. Worth scores "some ability" and "low" on
the two factors involved. Relative to his job as Sales
Supervisor, some skill improvement is indicated. However,
in another sales zone or if assigned to a different
product line, the skill assessment would have to be re-
interpreted in the light of the requirements of these new
job areas. The point of the assessment analysis is to
highlight exactly those areas that need strengthening.
Thus, if Mr. Worth wants to be considered eventually for
promotion to Assistant Sales Manager, he needs to develop
skills in two planning areas aside from consideration of
the other functional requirements of his current
assignment. After this individual needs assessment, a
developmental program combining both on-the-job training
and formal education can be designed for John Louis Worth.

Needs Analysis and CMO

In organizations where needs analysis is done as a
part of general career counseling, the purpose is to give
individual support in career focusing but to make no
commitment by the organization for a future job. Needs
analysis carried out in a CMO framework does target an
occupational or functional area or a specific future job.
Unexpected changes, however, can alter these plans. For
instance, business conditions could change, plans for a
divisional transfer could fall through, or a person may
decide not to retire early. In such cases, an individual
being developed for a blocked position may be placed in
some other suitable position. Some companies use training
classifications and "assistant" positions to meet these
contingencies as well as to ease transitions between jobs.

==

DEVELOPMENTS IN JOB INFORMATION

Building the Information Base

When attempting to develop a work analysis system, an organization should first build a base of reliable and useful job-related information. One way of doing this is to develop a basic set of skills commonly found in organization jobs. For example, one company formed a study team that identified necessary skills for all salaried jobs. These skills were sorted into five categories:

1. Managerial

   * leadership

   * developing/planning

   * supervisory

   * human relations

   * innovation

   * research/analyzing

2. Communications

   * instruction

   * writing

   * influence/persuasion

   * verbal

3. Work processing

   * detail, follow through

   * numerical

===

4. Physical

    * dexterity

    * strength

5. Developmental

    * learning

    * creativity

The study team provided definitions of these terms and in connection with supervisors and job holders, determined the importance of these skills for each job (i.e., degree of expertise in use). They then indicated the sources -- education, training, and/or type of work experience -- for gaining these skills. The same list of work skills describing job requirements were subsequently used to develop an EMPLOYEE SKILL PROFILE. Each skill was judged according to an individual's proficiency through self-rating and appraisals by the individual's supervisor. Additionally, the framework was established for the employee to describe systematically the type of work or job they would like to focus on for career purposes. Correspondingly, the company had a systematic basis then to respond to inquiries of employees. This coordinated activity involving CMO and individual career planning thus enhances both.

Accuracy and Application

    The accuracy of work and needs analyses is constantly threatened by changing work environments, technology, and people. Even so, techniques that can produce workable levels of accuracy are available. Using the tools outlined here (and more specifically in Burack and Mathys, Career Management in Organizations) one can reasonably identify job skills and specify appropriate training. Unfortunately, we know less about transferability of skills and the individual determination that can bridge skill deficiencies or bring into use alternate skill capabilities. Thus, it is important to use caution when analyzing skill identifications and assessments or proscribing areas of individual competency; results must be applied in thoughtful fashion with enough flexibility provided to accommodate these limitations. It is better to assign job responsibilities that give people a chance to perform rather than block them because we "know" they can't perform.

===

APPENDIX

Discussion Questions and Issues

1.   The general manager of a firm we visited indicated that they were going to move forward with their human resource program, OPPORTUNITY, even though they knew that many job descriptions needed updating.   Your comment?

2.   The learning styles of individuals often differ greatly.   How might this consideration affect a management development program incorporating the results of needs analysis?

3.   A medium-sized bank launched the first phase of its career planning program that consisted of updating its job analysis information.   The decision was made to "modernize" existing job descriptions ("responsibilities") rather than develop information on end job behaviors.   The head of the job analysis section felt that conventional job descriptions were more than adequate for the bank's management development program and that the added cost of developing "end-behavior" information was not justified.   What is your opinion?

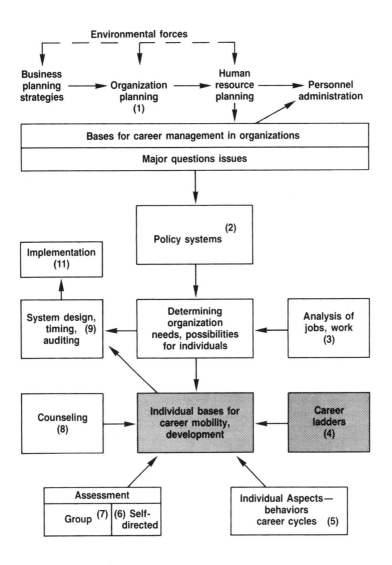

Environmental forces

Business planning strategies → Organization planning (1) → Human resource planning → Personnel administration

Bases for career management in organizations

Major questions issues

Policy systems (2)

Implementation (11)

System design, timing, (9) auditing ← Determining organization needs, possibilities for individuals ← Analysis of jobs, work (3)

Counseling (8) → Individual bases for career mobility, development ← Career ladders (4)

Assessment

| Group (7) | (6) Self-directed |

Individual Aspects— behaviors career cycles (5)

Chapter Four

Career Ladders: Concepts and Construction

CHAPTER FOUR

CAREER LADDER PROCEDURES

    Models of Career Ladders

        The traditional approach

        The career ladder approach

        The career lattice approach

    Work Analysis in Constructing Career Ladders

APPLICATION OF CAREER LADDER MODELS

    Industrial Applications: Traditional Approach

    Career Ladders in a Retailing Firm

    Pre-employment Career Analysis

    Pennsylvania's "Career Tree"

    Bank Application

Exhibit 4-1: The Career Tree of Government Jobs,
               Commonwealth of Pennsylvania

APPENDIX

    Discussion Questions and Issues

CAREER LADDERS: CONCEPTS AND CONSTRUCTIONS

CAREER LADDER PROCEDURES

An organization cannot be all things to all people, but it can provide information to help people make realistic career choices. For example, suppose a talented individual has just entered an organization. How does this person determine her organizational possibilities? How realistic are her perceptions? Or suppose an engineer is progressing in a company's engineering department but wants to get into line management or an operations department. Does he have to start from the bottom, or are there other options? Information on career ladders can help both these people by answering questions about individual opportunities and organizational career structures.

As a new understanding of jobs, work systems, and individual abilities develops, possibilities for job mobility are being formally defined and expanded. CAREER LADDERS represent the paths by which people move between jobs, positions, departments, or divisions of the organization. For the individual, career ladders channel career movement toward personal goals. For the organization, career ladders reflect efficient routes for skill development and also prescribe movement patterns valued highly in the organization. Career ladders help to bridge departments or units and so facilitate mobility in many directions within the organization.

Models of Career Ladders

There are three approaches to the development of career ladders in organizations.

==

   The traditional approach. Still the most basic and
widely used, this approach examines traditional channels
for promotions.   It is usually oriented to specific
departments or functional areas and concerned primarily
with vertical movements.   Since these career ladders tend
to be narrowly defined, advancement is often restricted to
jobs similar in title or description.
   An important question to ask about the traditional
approach, however, is whether traditional ladders should
still be favored today, given such rapidly changing
conditions that characterize most organizations.   Newer
approaches, like those discussed below, use new data and
methods to locate career channels that greatly supplement
the traditional ones.

   The career ladder approach.   This model groups
together jobs that have similar activities or end
behaviors.   The creation of these job clusters is, of
course, dependent on modern work analyses defining jobs in
terms of end behaviors (as discussed in the previous
chapter).   Once positions with related skills are
identified, lateral or diagonal connection between them
become clear, and thus mobility is facilitated.   This
becomes important as technology changes or departmental
personnel   needs   fluctuate.   For   instance,
interdepartmental transfers can greatly reduce the need to
hire or lay off people.
   A necessary step in this approach is to discard a
heavy reliance on job title, for titles alone do not
describe jobs.   The tasks performed by clerks, for
instance, vary from one organization to another, so it is
necessary to define exactly what a clerk does in a
particular job.

   The career lattice approach.   An extension of the
career ladder idea, the lattice model concentrates on the
interrelationships of career channels.   This approach
develops connections along lateral, diagonal, and vertical
lines of an organization, and so requires much more
information than the other two approaches.   Moreover, the
lattice model requires a greater commitment from the
organization to meet requirements of both formal career
management and individual career planning.   (An example of

===

a career lattice is found in Exhibit 4-1 at the end of this chapter).

Work Analysis in Constructing Career Ladders

Career ladders assist in locating connections between jobs for which related skills may not at first be obvious. But this depends first of all on accurate work analysis defining jobs in behavioral terms. Consider, for example, a potential employee transfer from sales to purchasing in one company. Behaviorally anchored statements from the work analysis would be used to construct a career ladder between these two departments in the following ways.

1. The work statements reveal responsibility of sales personnel in "establishing specifications," "planning requirements," and "authorizing special production;" correspondingly, work statements for one group of purchasing agents indicate "work with customer specifications and carrying out economic lot size calculations related to customer requirements."

2. Areas of shared responsibility between the two departments suggest possibilities for training and retraining.

3. Job clusters are identified on the basis of behavior, not job titles.

Once the basic character of needed skills or behaviors in purchasing and sales are identified, career ladders between them become more apparent. And by building more lateral mobility into the system, an organization has thus expanded internal growth possibilities.

==

APPLICATION OF CAREER LADDER MODELS

Industrial Application: Traditional Approach

Many organizations have not fully exploited information from their own records for constructing career ladders. For example, by analyzing past information and experience, a manufacturing firm developed a structure of career ladders that opened up new possibilities for jobs. Specifically, the firm compared lower-level positions according to the degree of education and former work experience an employee had. While inexperienced people started as plant crew, those with some clerical experience entered as stock clerks, and vocationally trained high school graduates were maintenance helpers. College graduates usually began in higher, management-level positions. Such analysis of company records, by identifying specific entry points for new hires thus shows ways to increase opportunities among lower-level personnel. They also closely examined jobs as to the types of work experience that favored particular jobs and those that supported mobility or promotion. Of particular interest were "exceptional" or "unusual" transfers of people that indicated possibilities for skill transferability. For example, depending on his or her ability, a plant crew person could become a storekeeper, maintenance helper, or operator. In addition, this information also reveals that certain positions are critical junctions where decisions about an employee's future moves are made. Career ladders nail down specific considerations -- e.g., electrical experience needed by maintenance helpers -- for such job decisions.

Career Ladders in a Retailing Firm

One retailing firm generated new information specifically for career ladders, as opposed to using existing company records exclusively. First of all, analysts identified all major job classifications on the following bases:

*   function (e.g., buyer, store manager)

===

*   store size (class 1, class 2, etc.), and

*   location (urban, rural, suburban).

Next, analysts traced promotion paths that naturally
occurred within a major job classification. For example,
"store manager, class 2 store (urban)" to "store manager,
class 1 store (urban)" to "store manager, class 2 store
(rural)." But this analysis, although revealing some
moves not thought likely before, included quite a wide
span of salaries. So, to supplement their new data, the
analysts used existing information from their job
evaluation and salary system (the Hay Plan). In this way,
both new and old paths of personnel movement can be seen
in the context of the overall salary structure to explain
past bases for promotion and to suggest possibilities for
better lateral mobility. Subsequently, many new paths
were opened up as training slots to improve personnel
assignment and to further affirmative action goals as
well.

Pre-employment Career Analysis (at Atlantic-Richfield)

A final example of a career ladder involves pre-
employment practices. As part of their recruiting effort,
Atlantic-Richfield acquaints college entrants with charts
showing job movement in many areas -- e.g., marketing,
engineering, manufacturing, and accounting. This pre-
employment strategy lets potential employees determine for
themselves how their college preparation fits with company
structure.

Pennsylvania's "Career Tree"

A career lattice (or matrix) is an extension of the
career ladder approach and results in a comprehensive
model for employee skill development and mobility. A
lattice or "career tree" developed by the Commonwealth of
Pennsylvania offers a good example (see Exhibit 4-1). The
career tree indicates points of entry into the job
structure and the many ways -- lateral, vertical, diagonal

EXHIBIT 4-1:   The Career Tree of Government Jobs, Commonwealth of Pennsylvania

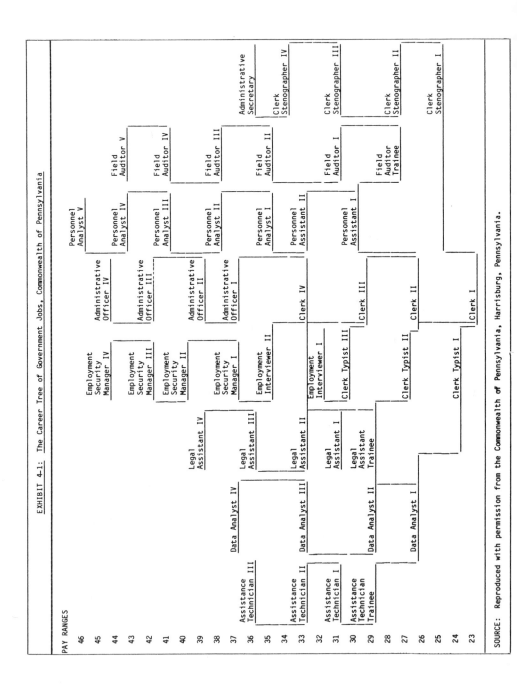

SOURCE: Reproduced with permission from the Commonwealth of Pennsylvania, Harrisburg, Pennsylvania.

==

-- of advancing individual careers. The information provided by this analysis is also used by line supervisors and counselors to help employees identify skills, experience, and educational requirements for each job.

Bank Application

Manufacturers Hanover Trust Bank in New York developed a system called "Human Resource Matrixing" for its computer operations. It is a comprehensive program for hiring and promotion based on specific skills and employee performance. Career ladders define the relationships among positions and identify key areas of skill and knowledge. Then the bank went farther and worked out a skills matrix which categorizes skills and proficiency levels required for each position. Proficiency is rated on four levels: current training and exposure, moderate usage, heavy usage, and expert knowledge and usage. Most positions require proficiency in six of the eight skills groups. Skills that need to be learned are also identified.

===

APPENDIX

Discussion Questions and Issues

1. A regional department store chain identified a
    network of career ladders a part of a new career
    planning program. The firm's executive officers,
    however, had never formalized the company's position
    on career planning or the more comprehensive human
    resource planning and development. Your opinion of
    possible problems?

2. The transition from traditional paths of career
    movement to those of career ladders are said to
    create many new employee opportunities. Yet it
    must be acknowledged that, from a supervisory
    viewpoint, the newer pathways often lead to
    departments or functional units where the job
    applicant or transferee is seen as quite foreign
    relative to the one that customarily fills an
    available job slot. If in a given organization a
    "career ladder" network has been newly created, what
    is your opinion of problems likely to arise among
    "home" and "receiving" department supervisors and how
    should these be treated?

3. In your experience, what are some common skills or
    work behaviors among jobs you are acquainted with
    that otherwise have quite different job titles?

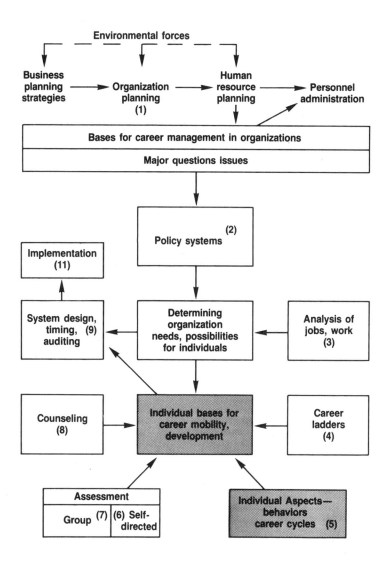

Chapter Five

Career Attitudes
and Behavior

CHAPTER FIVE

CAREER ATTITUDES

   Career Life Cycles

   Career Paths and Goals

   Exchange Between Employer and Employee

MEASURING INDIVIDUAL WORK NEEDS

   The Work Characteristics Form

   Department or Group Work Analysis

WORK AND JOB DESIGN FOR SATISFACTION AND PERFORMANCE

   Measuring Job Satisfaction

   Quality of Work Life - Job Enrichment

Exhibit 1-1:   Work Characteristics: Present and Desired
               Needs

Exhibit 5-2:   Plot of Need Areas for an Individual

Exhibit 5-3:   Analyzing Job Satisfaction and Assessing
               Behavioral Factors

APPENDIX

   Questions and Discussion Issues

CAREER ATTITUDES AND BEHAVIOR

INTRODUCTION

As explained at the beginning of this summary, one purpose of CMO is to relate individual career planning to the overall needs of the organization. But before this interplay can be effected, those involved in CMO need to understand how individuals function in career and behavioral terms within organizations and work systems.

People seek employment for a variety of reasons other than economic; the human urge for creation and enterprise as well as higher-order needs for achievement and recognition are some of the larger workings that make people get up to alarm clocks every morning. But once on the job, human behavior takes on more personal rhythms of particular needs and desires as individuals try to fit and grow within an organization. In this chapter, we will examine some ways of understanding human behavior in organized work systems: (1) how individuals see their jobs in relation to their lives, (2) how the organization affects an individual at critical phases of his or her development, and (3) the interplay of work, individual needs, performance, and work design.

CAREER ATTITUDES

Two key ideas -- the notion of career life cycles and that of exchange between employer and employee -- underlie all behavioral analysis regarding individuals and careers.

Career Life Cycles

Life-cycle theorists such as Erik Erickson, Roger

73

==

Gould, and George Vaillant see human development as taking
place in a characteristic pattern to the extent that
certain stages can be predicted. Thus, since a job plays
such an important part in anyone's life, many of those
involved in career planning think of careers as a
patterned process of stages happening over time, much of
which can not only be anticipated in a general range but
guided as well.

For example, in about their mid-twenties, most people
get their first full-time job which may take the form of
trial and error relative to career interests and
individual abilities. Often a mentor -- e.g., a
supervisor or seasoned professional associate -- provides
advice or support at this formative stage. Usually by the
late twenties or early thirties a person takes off
professionally either by changing jobs, being promoted to
more responsibility, or otherwise moving up. At this
point an individual gains self-confidence in his or her
abilities and career progress. Mid-career, in the
forties, is sometimes a period of mental trauma arising
from business pressures, increased personal
responsibilities, and/or psychological assessments of
one's progress so far. Some people may stagnate or even
decline at this time, while others go on to new heights
and personal fulfillment. Yet there is nothing automatic
about human development taking place in a progressive
manner. Individuals and careers may get side-tracked for
years or permanently.

Another influence on career life cycles are recent
social and economic changes that have altered traditional
family relationships and the composition of the work force
as well. More people have dual-career marriages these
days, which, especially if children are involved, affect
such considerations as job transfers to another area or
time off for vacations or personal days.

Women who have been out of the work force for 10 to
15 years to raise children often confront the same first-
job questions as did new employees in their twenties. In
addition, many women trained for traditional roles, such
as teaching or nursing, often seek different occupations
in business or administration.

Similarly, legislation dealing with equal employment,
comprehensive employment and training (CETA), and the

==

handicapped, for example, has brought people into the work force who were formerly disadvantaged by race, sex, handicap or poverty.
All these changes in the composition of the work force have contributed to more multiple (changed) careers, dual careers, and new careers. A career can no longer be seen as a static occupation. In a changing world, people require changes. In fact, a survey of various professional groups indicate that having three or four radically different occupations before age 50 is increasingly common.

Career Paths and Goals

A somewhat different orientation from seeing careers as part of life cycles, the PATH GOAL approach emphasizes motivation regarding specific goals. It is based on the EXPECTANCY THEORY of career progress in which individuals make choices from among a given set of alternatives. A path-goal orientation provides a logical framework for viewing careers: career goals, methods of achievement, alternatives, and the likelihood of realizing valued goals, potency of particular choices (relative value), and choices. In this way, an individual's long-term career goals can dictate certain short-term decisions. Moreover, individuals can evaluate their current situation in relation to long-term career goals. A major benefit of career thinking in a path-goal framework is that it keeps an individual focused on plans for the future in addition to present needs and desires. This approach also encourages systematic thinking regarding one's career.
The following are some specific steps in path-goal modelling.

1.   Identify career goals. These long-range accomplishments are likely to be quite broad in nature: good family life, economic security, professional recognition, executive responsibilities, for example.

2.   Set objectives. Objectives are more specific than goals in timing and detail. For instance,

==

an MBA degree may be seen as a way to achieve economic security, prestige, or executive responsibility.

3. **Find the means.** These are specific ways, such as enrolling in a continuing education course or transfering jobs, to secure an objective.

4. **Consider alternatives.** People make many career choices throughout their lives from among the alternatives offered -- e.g., whether to transfer to another geographical area, to change jobs within an organization, or to take a job with another organization.

5. **Judge efficiency.** The efficiency of an alternative can be viewed in two ways: (a) objectively, as costs, time, benefits, and (b) subjectively, as convenience, amount of stress, fear of failure, family welfare, personal satisfaction.

Ultimately, career choices are much more complicated than these steps imply. Because there are often so many variables to consider -- career and life goals as well as multiple alternatives -- a clear-cut decision is impossible. Most often a compromise is reached: one might defer life goals (marriage) to choose the means (two years of traveling) for attaining career goals (professional advancement). On the other hand, another person might postpone career goals to start a family. Counseling and reality-checking with associates provides valuable help in addressing these career issues. A full discussion of counseling is in Chapter 8.

Exchange Between Employer and Employee

So far we have focused primarily on satisfying an individual's career needs. However, the organization also seeks to satisfy a number of needs through its recruitment and employment practices. Inasmuch as both individuals and the organization speculate on future development,

==

contributions, and opportunities, they are locked in an exchange relationship that changes over time. Initially, the exchange between employer and employee is tangible: the individual thinks about the nature of the job, salary, benefits, location, and company reputation, while the company scrutinizes an individual's accomplishments as proven by his or her education and work experience. In the long run, though, an organization is in the position to offer an individual many career opportunities, as we have seen. Individuals in turn bring ingenuity, creativity, and other human qualities to a company that are good not only for the company's continued growth but for its image as well.

MEASURING INDIVIDUAL WORK NEEDS

Just as individual needs have an important impact on career work objectives, they also affect the design of jobs and work systems. Of interest here is the possible difference a job holder sees between present work features and those desired in the future. People's requirements change over time in response to maturing and all kinds of external developments and internal organizational changes. Also, many people find themselves in situations that fall short of their expectations.

A number of instruments have been developed to help translate personal needs into aspects of work and jobs. These instruments are not perfect and at best only add to our understanding. But since they combine analysis of both behavior and work, the results of these instruments can provide the basis for job design and enrichment. The WORK CHARACTERISTICS FORM is one of these newer, useful instruments.

The Work Characteristics Form

This instrument is composed of twenty-one statements that are then divided into seven job-need areas (see Exhibit 5-1). Individuals rate the degree to which each statement describes their current and desired jobs, coming up with two separate scores for each of the seven areas.

EXHIBIT 5-1: Work Characteristics: Present and Desired Needs

PART I:

Put an x in the box after each statement that best describes characteristics of (a)
your current job and (b) the type of job you would like to have.

VALUE SCALE
1 = none at all   2 = some   3 = moderate amount   4 = quite a bit   5 = a great deal

		current job 1 2 3 4 5	desired job 1 2 3 4 5
1.	Responsiblity and authority over others at work.	□ □ □ □ □	□ □ □ □ □
2.	Opportunity to make decisions about my work.	□ □ □ □ □	□ □ □ □ □
3.	Work variety.	□ □ □ □ □	□ □ □ □ □
4.	A sense of accomplishment.	□ □ □ □ □	□ □ □ □ □
5.	Job security.	□ □ □ □ □	□ □ □ □ □
6.	Having friendly people with whom to work.	□ □ □ □ □	□ □ □ □ □
7.	Recognition (importance) accorded me by organization.	□ □ □ □ □	□ □ □ □ □
8.	Supervision and leadership.	□ □ □ □ □	□ □ □ □ □
9.	Chance to deal regularly with changing situations.	□ □ □ □ □	□ □ □ □ □
10.	Some opportunity to do things on my own.	□ □ □ □ □	□ □ □ □ □
11.	Use of my best talents and abilities at work.	□ □ □ □ □	□ □ □ □ □
12.	Regular payroll check.	□ □ □ □ □	□ □ □ □ □
13.	Cordial relations with others at work.	□ □ □ □ □	□ □ □ □ □
14.	Pride in my work.	□ □ □ □ □	□ □ □ □ □
15.	Taking responsibility for the work of others.	□ □ □ □ □	□ □ □ □ □
16.	Chance to try out my own ideas at work.	□ □ □ □ □	□ □ □ □ □
17.	Flexibility regarding how my job is done.	□ □ □ □ □	□ □ □ □ □
18.	Opportunity to expand talents and abilities at work.	□ □ □ □ □	□ □ □ □ □

EXHIBIT 5-1: Work Characteristics: Present and Desired Needs (cont'd)

	current job 1 2 3 4 5	desired job 1 2 3 4 5
19. Dependence of people on me for guidance.	⬜⬜⬜⬜⬜	⬜⬜⬜⬜⬜
20. Opportunity and need to cooperate with others at work.	⬜⬜⬜⬜⬜	⬜⬜⬜⬜⬜
21. Supervisor acknowledges me for doing a good job.	⬜⬜⬜⬜⬜	⬜⬜⬜⬜⬜

PART II: Steps.

1. For each need area add the points you received on each statement in Part I. Enter totals for current and desired job. Note: Maximum score is 15 for any need area.

2. Plot your scores on a graph. (See Exhibit 5-2.)

3. Compare current and desired need categories.

   a. Which areas are really important to you?

   b. Where are the greatest deficiencies?

   c. Are there high priority areas for you?

		TOTAL POINTS	
NEED AREA	STATEMENT NUMBER	CURRENT	DESIRED
•Security	5, 12, 19	_____	_____
•Sense of belonging	6, 13, 20	_____	_____
•Recognition (esteem)	7, 14, 21	_____	_____
•Variety	3, 9, 17	_____	_____
•Autonomy	2, 10, 16	_____	_____
•Responsibility	1, 8, 15	_____	_____
•Use of abilities	4, 11, 18	_____	_____

SOURCE: Based on ideas discussed in Elmer H. Burack and Robert D. Smith, Personnel Management: A Human Resource Systems Approach (New York, N.Y.: John Wiley & Sons, 1982), Elmer H. Burack and Nicholas J. Mathys, Career Management in Organizations: A Practical Human Resource Planning Approach (Lake Forest, IL: Brace Park Press, 1980), and analyses of various behavioral scientists including Lyman Porter, Frederick Herzberg, and members of the Telemetrics International Organization.

EXHIBIT 5-2: Plot of Need Areas for an Individual

Points

15														
14														
13														
12														
11														
10														
9														
8														
7														
6														
5														
4														
3														
2														
1														

c   d   c   d   c   d   c   d   c   d   c   d   c   d

Security   Belonging   Recognition   Variety   Autonomy   Responsibility   Use of ability

KEY: _____ = current job   o = current job
        _ _ _ _   = desired job |⁻| = desired job

SOURCE: Based on ideas discussed in Elmer H. Burack and Robert D. Smith, Personnel Management: A Human Resource Systems Approach (New York, N.Y.: John Wiley & Sons, 1982), Elmer H. Burack and Nicholas J. Mathys, Career Management in Organizations: A Practical Human Resource Planning Approach (Lake Forest, IL: Brace Park Press, 1980), and analyses of various behavioral scientists including Lyman Porter, Frederick Herzberg, and members of the Telemetrics International Organization.

==

When these scores are plotted on a graph (Exhibit 5-2), the discrepancy between current and desired job becomes clear.

The results of this job audit can be used in several ways:

* The organization can track changes in aspirations and work views over time.

* Results can help set work design goals, when it is determined that problems exist in an organization.

* Individuals can use the audit format to sharpen their own thinking about career plans.

Usually the values for the current job-need plot are below the desired job-need plot, suggesting that people invariably seek improvement in their current circumstances. Where a major divergence exists, however, job design or some type of specific career action is needed. On occasion the current job-need plot will be above the desired job-need plot, indicating that an employee wants less of a work-related activity. In some cases, individuals may adjust to the reality of the job as they see it and reduce their expectations. Often the need plot will vary with type of occupation or level of responsibility. Managerial and professional jobs usually have higher scores on need areas 3 through 7, than do clerical or blue collar jobs.

Department or Group Work Analysis

At times, work characteristics forms and graphs are used with groups of employees to identify general points of dissatisfaction or to isolate specific problems. One architectural/engineering firm used the forms to analyze the reasons for high turnover among young people and much tension among engineers, architects, and staff. The results of these studies are too complex to discuss here. But some specific problems that emerged were as follows: (1) lack of career mobility, challenge, and recognition,

(2) need to update credentials of senior professionals who
were often behind in the latest technological advances,
and (3) need for career ladders for office staff, mostly
women, who were often over-qualified for their jobs.

WORK AND JOB DESIGN FOR SATISFACTION AND PERFORMANCE

Much of today's job redesign and enrichment work is
based on studies by Abraham Maslow, who analyzed behavior
in terms of a "hierarchy of needs," and Frederick
Herzberg, who emphasized "motivational" factors in human
behavior. Thus, career analysts recognize that what
people do on the job has a major bearing on their sense of
well-being, interest in the organization, job
satisfaction, and performance. Consequently, aspects of
job satisfaction are materially related to absenteeism and
turnover, cooperation, identification with organization
interests, loyalty, and dependability.

Path-goal models and work characteristics forms can
help individuals get particular job information to assess
and direct their career progress. This section examines
how an organization can systematically measure features of
general employee satisfaction and design jobs that better
respond to employee needs. The approaches involve groups
as well as individuals.

Factors affecting work-related satisfaction involve
the general organizational climate as well as job
assignment and procedures and the job itself.

For example, more general organizational
considerations include:

*   a sense of expectations of career possibilities
     or achieving desired work features based on
     recruiting or early work experience,

*   fulfillment of company promises or implied
     benefits,

*   congeniality of work environment,

*   employment stability, and

===

*   salary and benefits structure.

More specific work-related factors involving job and person include:

*   work variety or diversity,

*   recognition for accomplishments,

*   ability to make meaningful decisions,

*   being in command of the relevant knowledge and skills in comparison to job demands,

*   feedback on work program and performance results,

*   participation in setting meaningful work objectives, and

*   fit of individual work style and job characteristics.

The design or redesign of work situations or jobs can only deal realistically with some of these many elements, yet a change in one or two areas may be seen by the individual as significant in his or her scheme of things.

Measuring Job Satisfaction

Since there are so many variables governing work-related satisfaction on one's job, no single factor can be isolated and measured. The JOB DESCRIPTION INDEX (JDI), developed by Patricia Smith and her associates, is one test of job satisfaction that covers five areas.

1.   Work: amount of challenge, creativity, responsibility, etc.

2.   Pay: adequacy of salary in relation to work performed.

3.   Promotion: opportunity, frequency, as well as
     possibility.

4.   Supervision: competency, amiability, and
     honesty in dealings with subordinates.

5.   Co-workers: loyalty and congeniality of work
     group.

The JDI, as well as other attitudinal tests is most
successful identifying TRENDS rather than absolute values.
The ability to track trends over time, however, can
measure the effectiveness of particular managerial
actions. This is an important application of action
research regarding personnel matters and also one
achieving a degree of regularity in many enterprises.

Overall, managerial intent in using testing
instruments is a basic consideration. Unless officials
are prepared to change a given work situation, initiating
a survey program can do more harm than good. Asking
employees to state their grievances raises their
expectations of reform, which if disappointed can produce
more frustration or dissatisfaction than ever before.

Quality of Work Life - Job Enrichment

Instruments such as the JDI and work characteristics
forms that help identify elements of satisfaction and
dissatisfaction on the job provide a data base for quality
of work life studies. Central to this fast-growing area
of interest are studies to improve the work situation and
the job itself. Exhibit 5-3 shows a two-part form to help
obtain such data. The first portion analyzes the elements
affecting job satisfaction, and the other points out
specific behavioral characteristics of the work situation
and the job. Those involved in assessing this data must
then ask themselves two basic questions:

*   Does the work situation or job appear to be low
     in "enriching" factors?

*   Are there practical ways to improve these

EXHIBIT 5-3: Analyzing Job Satisfaction and Assessing Behavioral Factors

PART I: Select a job and (a) identify those aspects you feel affect job satisfaction/ dissatisfaction the most, (b) tell why they are important, and (c) suggest ways to improve job satisfaction.

JOB:_____

(a) Major factors affecting job satisfaction	(b) Why factors are important	(c) How to improve
_____	_____	_____
_____	_____	_____
_____	_____	_____
_____	_____	_____
_____	_____	_____
_____	_____	_____
_____	_____	_____

PART II: For the same job, estimate its relative content on key behavioral factors.

VALUE SCALE   1 = Much   5 = Little

                                                                        1 2 3 4 5

1. Autonomy: typically, how much is present? ☐ ☐ ☐ ☐ ☐

2. Work closure: how much of the whole task(s) does job involve? ☐ ☐ ☐ ☐ ☐

3. Variety: is there opportunity to do different things? How frequently are they done? ☐ ☐ ☐ ☐ ☐

4. Job significance in company, society, or stature among other people? ☐ ☐ ☐ ☐ ☐

5. Ability of supervisor to support the performance of job holders? ☐ ☐ ☐ ☐ ☐

6. Factors in job signaling good or poor performance of job holders? ☐ ☐ ☐ ☐ ☐

7. Challenge offered by job? ☐ ☐ ☐ ☐ ☐

8. Opportunity for initiative or creativity? ☐ ☐ ☐ ☐ ☐

9. Does job improve skills, allow for advancement to other jobs, and do career ladders exist? ☐ ☐ ☐ ☐ ☐

10. Opportunity to develop relationships with co-workers? ☐ ☐ ☐ ☐ ☐

11. Prestige, recognition associated with job outside organization? ☐ ☐ ☐ ☐ ☐

12. Flexibility in job techniques or performance approaches? ☐ ☐ ☐ ☐ ☐

Job enrichment potential (sum of content values ÷ 12): _____ ÷ 12 = _____

Maximum score = 5, most potential for improvement
Minimum score = 1, least potential for improvement

SOURCE: Adapted from Richard W. Beatty and Craig E. Schneier, Personnel Administration: An Experiential Skill-Building Approach (Reading, MA: Addison-Wesley, 1977), pp. 369-87.

factors?

These situations must be approached on an experimental basis since (many) adjustments will have to be made for outcomes for which there is little history to go on.

There are steps involved in any job enrichment process that roughly assume the following order.

1. Initiate action research to study closely the people and the work situation, including estimated time and cost of an enrichment program. Also, action research is necessary to establish a monitoring mechanism for taking periodic readings.

2. Identify areas of potential job enrichment.

3. Select particular work areas as the site for an installation.

4. Gain the active cooperation and support of supervisors and workers interested in a quality of work life "experiment."

5. Study job procedures carefully for possible improvements.

6. Review personnel records and interview organization members

    Individuals must

    a. value the enrichment features being discussed,

    b. evidence desire to cooperate in installation, and

    c. show potential to benefit from improvements.

7. Install enrichment program.

==

8.   Do more action research to check progress and measure improvement.

It must be remembered that quality of work life "experiments" such as job enrichment are complex procedures depending on types of jobs and people involved as well as the nature of the organization. Some people may not particularly want their jobs "enriched," for various personal or professional reasons. In addition, certain technologies or procedures simply do not lend themselves to change, at least in the short run, or cannot be modified economically. For a more detailed and varied analysis of job enrichment and forms for such use, see the Appendix to Chapter 5 of Burack and Mathys, **Career Management in Organizations.**

APPENDIX

Discussion Questions and Issues

1. A firm involved with human resource planning has not
    included provisions for individual career planning.
    Officers are fearful that adding to this career
    component would encourage turnover.   Your view
    regarding this?

2. To what extent can supervisory leadership and
    activities directly affect factors identified with
    improvement in the work situation or job?   That is,
    what factors can be viewed as variables in terms of
    the work content and job insofar as supervisory
    actions are concerned?

3. In a quality of work life study, many line
    supervisors expressed doubt as to the practicality of
    the program.   Yet, because of employee pressures,
    management decided to move ahead with revamping job
    procedures.   The subsequent installation proved to be
    a failure and was discontinued after about six
    months. Supervisors were blamed for "torpedoing" the
    program. What is your view on selling a quality of
    work life/job enrichment program?

4. A company study in an electronics firm using the
    "work characteristics form" indicated a strong desire
    on the part of engineers for more challenging work
    relative to their current assignments.   How would you
    propose dealing with this situation?

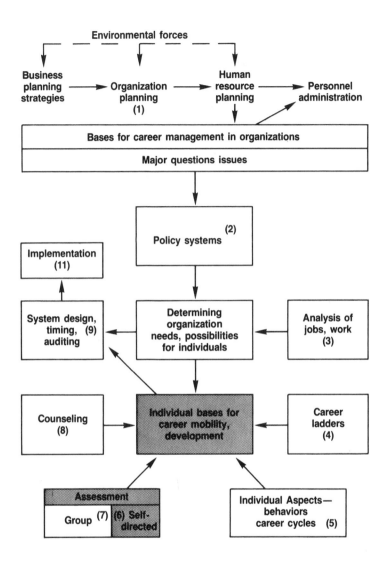

Environmental forces

Business planning strategies → Organization planning (1) → Human resource planning → Personnel administration

Bases for career management in organizations

Major questions issues

Policy systems (2)

Implementation (11)

System design, timing, (9) auditing

Determining organization needs, possibilities for individuals

Analysis of jobs, work (3)

Counseling (8)

Individual bases for career mobility, development

Career ladders (4)

Assessment

Group (7) (6) Self-directed

Individual Aspects— behaviors career cycles (5)

Chapter Six

Individual Assessment and Career Pathing

CHAPTER SIX

INDIVIDUAL ASSESSMENT: THE ORGANIZATIONAL ROLE

   Feedback

   Review Systems: The National Stores Experience

   Assessment of High Potentials: The USDA Experience

SELF-ASSESSMENT AND CAREER PATHING

   Self-Assessment Exercises

   Charting Goals

      "Who Am I?"

      Career path exercise

      Career planning workbook

      Workshop format

   Toward an Integrated System: Century Business Sales

   Exhibit 6-1: Performance Factors Used for Identification
                 of High Potential

   Exhibit 6-2: Steps Toward an Individual Development
                 Program

APPENDIX

   Discussion Questions and Issues

INDIVIDUAL ASSESSMENT AND CAREER PATHING

INDIVIDUAL ASSESSMENT: THE ORGANIZATIONAL ROLE

Traditional assessment relies mainly on the immediate supervisor's judgment of an individual's work performance (a "one on one" system). Too often such judgments are based on personality rather than merit and past behavior rather than potential. As a result, many errors can be made regarding promotions; mobility of competent people may be blocked; and people can be overlooked because of racial or sexual prejudice. Both the individual and the organization suffer in such situations; the organization because it may deny a potentially valuable employee or make a poor personnel decision and the individual because his or her talents may be thwarted.

Feedback

One way to rectify some of the shortcomings of traditional approaches is to give an employee accurate and timely feedback from the assessment process. It is common practice in many organizations for supervisors to give the individuals being assessed the results in written form. Disagreements can be discussed at this point and frequently resolved. The employee then signs the assessment form, signaling his or her acknowledgment of its content.

Although giving an employee feedback in this way is beneficial, it does not go far enough. One of the problems of these assessment procedures is that past performance is often given priority in future promotion opportunity. An important improvement in this system of individual assessment and feedback is the growing incorporation of performance factors and behavioral-type

==

items found to be important to higher managerial levels. Thus the assessment process is conducted in two parts; the first judges past performance and accomplishments against specific objectives; and the second assesses performance potential against a set of general managerial factors and behaviors. Judgments regarding future potential thus involve aspects of the individual and his or her work that often are not part of performance appraisals or that are only incompletely considered.

Review Systems: The National Stores Experience

Newer approaches to assessment involve a redesign of "one on one" systems and substantial changes in procedures. One such approach is the creation of a REVIEW COMMITTEE that includes higher-level management. This committee acts as a center for auditing, review, and decision making, while at the same time, serving as a clearing house to settle disputes in transfer, promotion, or training. The change instituted by National Stores illustrate the benefits of multiple judgments in the review committee structure. Several years ago, top management at National Stores decided to strengthen their ability to develop key people to fill or back up critical company positions. What they needed was a process to identify high-potential and succession candidates (for officer and senior management positions).

Toward this end, National Stores set up a committee of top executives to assess semi-annually the performance of a "talent pool" composed of some 250 employees. The review committee identified "feeder positions" -- i.e., those jobs thought good for preparatory training -- and key positions underlying the feeder network.

The long-term effects of this structure gave National Stores more control over succession and a stable development program. Moreover, the semi-annual review process committed senior management for the first time to a major role in career planning and development of potential officers.

===

Assessment of High Potentials: The USDA Experience

Substantive changes in the content and design of assessment depend to a large extent on extensive job analyses. An example of this process is provided by the U.S. Department of Agriculture.

As part of their management development effort, the USDA designed a 25-month executive development program for individuals with high potential. Unlike the case with National Stores, the candidates were people already in the upper levels of middle management who evidenced potential for top positions.

Nevertheless, the study team found that the previous list of job factors meant to apply generally to management positions was inadequately short. Thus, they enlarged the list and devised more particular job dimensions to be used in both assessments and performance appraisals. These performance factors (i.e., job dimensions) are listed in Exhibit 6-1: they were defined for specificity as well as for consistency. The USDA then used the assessments of potential (45 percent weighting) together with past performance appraisals (55 percent weighting) to determine acceptance of candidates into the executive development program.

In the long run, these types of performance factors (Exhibit 6-1) provide a flexible basis to judge future performance in a variety of work situations. They can also be used to judge adaptability of the individual to a particular job if they are supplemented with descriptive statements of that job.

SELF-ASSESSMENT AND CAREER PATHING

Self-assessment represents a useful new tool for career planning. Through self-diagnosis, individuals can actively join in the planning process and also reinforce information gathered in formal assessment procedures. It is at this point that individual career planning joins organization career management. For when carried out in a context of CMO, systematic self-assessment serves to provide important information regarding personal skills, interests, needs, and goals. This information, frequently

EXHIBIT 6-1: Performance Factors Used for Identification of High Potential

1. Oral communication skill: effectiveness of expression in individual or group situations.

2. Written communication skill: ability to express ideas clearly in writing in grammatical form.

3. Leadership: effectiveness in getting ideas accepted and in guiding a group or an individual to accomplish a task.

4. Interpersonal insight: skill in perceiving and reacting sensitively to the needs of others; objectivity in perceiving impact of self on others.

5. Planning and organization: ability to establish efficiently an appropriate course of action for self and/or others to accomplish a specific goal; ability to make appropriate use of human and fiscal resources.

6. Problem analysis: skill in identifying problems, securing relevant information, identifying possible causes of problems, and proposing alternative courses of action.

7. Stress tolerance: ability to perform under pressure or opposition.

8. Creativity: ability to generate, recognize, and/or accept imaginative solutions and innovations in management situations.

9. Decisiveness: ability to make decisions, render judgments, and take action or commit oneself.

10. Flexibility/adaptability: ability to modify behavioral style and management approach to reach a goal; ability to adapt to changing organizational needs and situations.

11. Decision making: ability to arrive at decisions through the appropriate use of logic or reason.

SOURCE: Internal Documents, U.S. Department of Labor. Reprinted with permission from Elmer H. Burack and Nicholas J. Mathys, Career Management in Organizations: A Practical Human Resource Planning Approach (Lake Forest, IL: Brace Park Press, 1980), p. 212.

deficient in personnel records, can contribute
significantly to assessment processes and, more generally,
CMO.
    Although self-assessment centers on the individual,
it is not conducted alone.

*   A supervisor can serve as a sounding board and
     reality check for employee notions of specific
     abilities and skills. He or she can also give
     informal assessments of an employee's sense of
     future job interests or skills utilization based
     on information solicited in self-assessment
     procedures.

*   Personnel specialists may serve in a formal
     counseling capacity to advise supervisors on CP
     policies or to back up the supervisor's
     counseling role with the employee.

*   Personnel counselors also provide factual data
     on occupations or specific data on opportunities
     elsewhere in the organization.

Self-Assessment Exercises

    The kind of self-assessment techniques used varies
depending upon the target group. For instance, if people
using an instrument have little experience in career
matters, a more factual and occupation-specific instrument
may be used. Sophisticated employees or those with
advanced degrees, who tend to be more competitive and
goal-oriented, may require a more detailed analysis.
Brief descriptions of some common instruments follow. But
regardless of what self-assessment procedure is used, line
managers, administrators, and career counselors must be
properly trained to provide needed information and to
utilize results where appropriate.

    Charting goals. This initial section has the purpose
of explaining the importance and means of developing goals
and general paths of action for achieving these. Thus,
this activity is both for skill building and initiating

==

the process of individual goal planning.

"Who Am I?"   The purpose of this exercise is to familiarize employees with the techniques commonly used to develop career plans: for a better understanding of themselves and their future goals.   It is an excellent point of departure for individual career thinking.   Some representative types of questions follow.

1.   To determine what you want to be doing in the future, write a short newspaper article about yourself five years from now.

2.   For the charts included determine your current position by assessing what you considered your major strengths and weaknesses, past and desired accomplishments, and values in personal and work life. (Several charts are provided that give definitions of many of these concepts and then provide for a patterned response).

3.   Write ten descriptive words or short phrases answering the question "Who am I?" and rank them in descending order of importance.

4.   List specific work-related career goals and the objectives by which to accomplish them.   Be sure to include:

a.   the resources to help achieve these goals,

b.   the barriers that might exist, and

c.   how barriers can be overcome.

5.   Develop a step-by-step diagram for achieving the goals previously stated.

Career path exercise.   Designed to improve one's skill in planning career paths, this exercise is more complicated than the previous one. Initially, an employee prepares a skill inventory that includes strengths and weaknesses on specific skills in technical, administrative, and managerial areas as well as in communication, social, and personal abilities. Next, the individual compiles a work sheet set up on a time grid which brings together information on jobs, skills, and experience from two viewpoints: past history and future possibilities.

Career planning workbook. As referenced in a previous chapter, one form of this material was developed by Atlantic-Richfield as part of its pre-employment processing. This workbook is designed specifically for college graduates considering a job at ARCO. The workbook includes information on key areas of employment and outlines typical career paths. Also included are areas for self-inquiry including:

*   past accomplishments,

*   abilities,

*   skills,

*   values,

*   importance of job factors (challenge, salary, etc.), and

*   importance of non-job factors (community, frequency of moves, climate, etc.

Workshop format. In an organization group, peers provide reality checking for self-assessment of skills, alternatives and plans that an individual working alone might miss. A typical format is divided into three major phases:

1. Self analysis of skills and desires.

2. Organizational analysis of short-term opportunities.

3. Action planning for self-development.

==

Toward An Integrated System: Century Business Sales

     The procedures developed by Century Business Sales, a
rapidly growing office equipment company, are similar to
those at other leading companies. This company example
also serves to illustrate important points that are raised
in this chapter:

*   How institutional policy establishes a climate
       for developing high-potential people.

*   The importance of jointly considering
       organizational, technical, human resource, and
       individual analyses.

*   The necessity of defining a common set of work
       performance factors in assessing potential and
       developing career programs.

     Even though Century Business Sales already had a
human resource planning system, top management was
concerned that the number of people being identified for
possible promotions was insufficient. Consequently, they
decided to develop a career planning system that would
richly supplement the existing information base.
     As part of the existing HR program, each manager kept
a workbook detailing potential job movement and
replacements for key positions. Prior to completing "the
book," as it is called, each manager made an annual review
of employee performance and development plans. A major
problem in the system, however, centered around individual
responses to management questions; "I want to get ahead"
or "I want to get into management" that were found to be
too general to be useful in sorting out specific career
needs.
     To remedy this problem, company researchers compiled
a detailed self-assessment instrument called the **personal
career audit.** The audit sheet focused on four skill areas
-- technical, communication, administrative, leadership --
and asked questions about current job, personal life, and
the future. At the end of the form, the employee was
asked to list at least ten action steps toward achieving
personally valued work goals.

===

When an employee completed the audit, he or she and the supervisor discussed it and agreed on the skills to include in "the book." Together they then devised a specific development program for the employee, complete with timetable (see Exhibit 6-2 for steps in the procedure). In this way, the supervisor served as a reality check on the employee's self-assessment as well as coach and developer.

Moreover, the personal audit sheet was made part of the annual review and development process to help managers keep abreast of current employee needs and career plans. For a reprint of the entire personal career audit, see Appendix B in Chapter 6 of Burack and Mathys, **Career Management in Organizations.**

One major criticism of the Century Business Sales program is its dependence on the immediate supervisor for individual review, unit planning, and the integration of this information. Individual talents may be missed or inequality in the selection may result from such a reliance on a supervisor's judgment. The existence of a mandatory review process at higher managerial levels helped to eliminate inequities in the modified career system design.

EXHIBIT 6-2:   Steps Toward an Individual Development Program

1. Individual completes career audit.

    2. Meets with supervisor and classifies questions.

        3. Career goals are summarized in "the book."

            4. Individual's ideas regarding development (both past
                experience and future plans) entered in "the book."

                5. Individual assesses   Supervisor assesses
                    personal skills.   individual's skills.

                    6. Joint discussion and agreement on skills to
                        include in "the book" and how to substantiate
                        them.

                        7. Supervisor reviews career plans, skills, and
                            appraisal date.

                            8. Then finalizes development plans with
                                individual.

                                9. Supervisor and individual meet to
                                    finalize program and set timetable.

SOURCE: Adapted from Elmer H. Burack and Nicholas J. Mathys,
Career Management in Organizations: A Practical Human Resource
Planning Approach (Lake Forest, IL: Brace Park Press, 1980), p. 231.

==

APPENDIX

Discussion Questions and Issues

1. Many firms still place primary emphasis for promotion on the person's past record of performance appraisals. Your viewpoint on this?

2. A manufacturer of computer equipment launched a pre-employment career assessment program in connection with its college recruiting of systems graduates. However, a company officer wanted the program dropped when he found out that visits to the company by candidates dropped 25 percent. In your view, was the officer justified in his recommendation?

3. General performance factors used in the identification of high potentials have been criticized by some managers for their use in connection with both administrative and technical types of jobs and people. What do you feel might be the limitations and strong features of this approach?

4. A large company claims that it identifies 25 percent more qualified supervisory candidates since starting its use of self-assessment career materials and a self-nomination process. What are some considerations that you feel might account for these results?

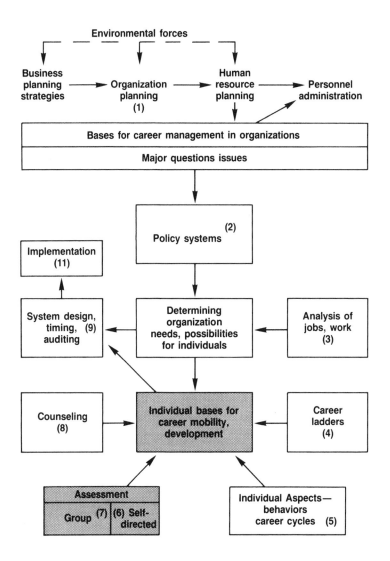

Chapter Seven

The Assessment Center

CHAPTER SEVEN

ASSESSMENT GROUPS

   Background

   Activities of Assessment Centers

   Using the Results of Group Assessments

   Reasons for Success of Assessment Center Techniques

ASSESSMENT CENTER OBJECTIVES

   Selection Approach

   Developmental Approach

Exhibit 7-1: Performance Factors Used for Group
              Assessments

APPENDIX

   Discussion Questions and Issues

THE ASSESSMENT CENTER

ASSESSMENT GROUPS

Background

Group assessment dates from World War I, when a similar procedure was used by the Germans to select officers. During World War II, the United States up-dated a number of techniques to evaluate personnel for special assignments behind enemy lines. Contemporary use, and subsequently the model for assessment centers in private industry, is attributed to the American Telephone and Telegraph Company (AT&T) in 1956. By the early 1960's, a growing number of companies such as IBM, General Electric, and J.C. Penney had begun using the assessment center for career development and planning. At the heart of the assessment center approach is a group of job or work dimensions that are common to many managerial functions or to the class of jobs for which people are being assessed.

The "assessment center" is often established in a particular facility but of much greater importance to note is that it represents a systematic process. A panel of well-trained assessors views and rates the performances of individual group members who perform a variety of work-related tasks. Early assessment centers required some four to five days for the group exercises and analyses by the assessors. Through careful research and a growing body of experience, the overall time required has been reduced to some two to three days. The results of assessment centers are now used for applicant selection, prescribing training and development needs, and judging potential for possible (future) promotions or transfers to different occupational areas. The assessment center is also used as a training technique in group processes, problem solving, decision making, and planning.

==

Activities of Assessment Centers

A major reason for growth of assessment centers is
that unlike traditional assessment of potential, this
group approach seeks out additional information beyond
appraisal of past performance as the basis for later
judgments. Thus there is a deliberate effort to avoid,
for example, promoting the best machine operator to
supervisor or the best salesperson to manager, simply
because of past performance. Instead, a series of
assessment center tasks focuses on job-related behavior to
predict future performance on a targeted job or in a more
general managerial activity.

To predict future job performance, assessment centers
put potential candidates through a variety of experiences
that utilize skills and abilities common to higher level
functions. By means of a JOB SIMULATION, a group of
employees performs certain activities found in the
targeted jobs, while specially trained managers for these
jobs and a professional coordinator observe and evaluate
them. Tasks performed during an assessment group are
uniformly administered, thereby ensuring greater accuracy.
In addition, since several assessors observe each
candidate, an opportunity for balanced judgment is better
assured. When carefully organized, the results of
assessment centers have been found to be job-related and
valid in numerous court cases.

Another factor accounting for greater accuracy in
this group assessment approach is the identification of
specific performance factors (job dimensions) to evaluate
managerial skills and abilities. An employee's
performance is rated on these specific dimensions.

Sets of performance factors vary in different
organizations, but include relatively common
characteristics needed for managerial jobs. Exhibit 7-1
lists seventeen performance dimensions developed by
Midwest Gas. Although this list is similar to the one for
individual assessment (Exhibit 6-1), the concepts are
refined by additional entries such as CAREER AMBITION and
breaking down of such categories as COMMUNICATION into
ORAL,   WRITTEN, PRESENTATION, and READING AND
UNDERSTANDING.

EXHIBIT 7-1: Performance Factors Used for Group Assessments

1. Oral communication skill: effectiveness of expression in individual or group situations.

2. Oral presentation skill: ability to make a persuasive, clear presentation of ideas or facts.

3. Written communication skill: ability to express ideas clearly in writing in grammatical form.

4. Stress tolerance: stability of performance under pressure and opposition; emotional stability.

5. Career ambition: motivation to advance to higher job levels.

6. Leadership: effectiveness in bringing an individual or a group to accomplish a task and in getting ideas accepted; motivating subordinates.

7. Sensitivity: skill in perceiving and reacting sensitively to the needs of others; listening skills.

8. Flexibility: ability to modify behavioral style and management approach to reach a goal; acceptance of change; ability to come up with unique solutions.

9. Tenacity: tendency to stay with a problem or line of thought until the matter is settled.

10. Independence: action based on personal convictions rather than a desire to please others; ability to administer discipline, enforce work roles, etc.

11. Planning and organization: effectiveness in planning and organizing own activities and those of a group.

12. Delegation and control: appropriateness and clarity of delegation; establishment of follow-up procedures; appreciation of need for control over processes.

13. Problem analysis: effectiveness in seeking out pertinent data and determining the source of others.

14. Judgment: ability to reach logical conclusions based on the evidence at hand.

15. Decisiveness: readiness to make decisions or to render judgment.

16. Reading and understanding: ability to read and comprehend work-related material such as company bulletins, union contracts, government regulations, etc.

17. Initiative: active efforts to influence events rather than passive acceptance; self-confidence; self-starter; ability to operate with minimum supervision.

SOURCE: Reprinted with permission from Elmer H. Burack and Nicholas J. Mathys, Career Management in Organizations: A Practical Human Resource Planning Approach (Lake Forest, IL: Brace Park Press, 1980), p. 279.

==

Using the Results of Group Assessments

Relatively few companies use the assessment center exclusively for determining promotion potential, although some organizations use it as a "go or no-go" assessment for promotion to first-level supervisor. Others use group assessment information to supplement performance appraisals in making career decisions. Increasingly, companies are using assessment centers for developmental purposes, especially for middle-level managers, because feedback from the assessors reaffirms individual abilities or suggests new areas of inquiry.

Reasons for Success of Assessment Center Techniques

Continued growth of the assessment center can be attributed to several considerations:

1. The technique is a major improvement over most in place previously in predicting success. Candidates chosen by this method are usually two to three times more successful at higher management levels than those promoted mostly on the basis of a supervisor's judgment.

2. Participation in the program has often been a powerful learning experience for both participants and assessors. A better understanding of a supervisor's job is usually an outcome.

3. Managers like assessment centers because the techniques are closely related to the challenges employees will face as they move up in management.

4. The data gathered for assessment exercises usually provide specific information on various performance factors. As a result, well-designed assessment centers have usually passed court tests related to equal employment and nondiscriminatory practices matters.

===

5. The results of assessment centers often provide
    inputs for management training and development
    programs and informal self-development programs.

ASSESSMENT CENTER OBJECTIVES

Although procedures are similiar among most
assessment centers, specific approaches may differ because
they are tailored to fit specific organizational
objectives. Examples of the use of an assessment center
as a selection and a developmental device follow.

Selection Approach

A large automobile manufacturer used the group
assessment approach to select first-level supervisors for
manufacturing, sales, and warehousing. For example, in
manufacturing, seven skill areas were identified as
important to the job, including planning, problem solving,
and interpersonal abilities. For all candidates, the
process was an accept or reject proposition: if results
were satisfactory, the candidate was placed on a waiting
list for supervisory openings. If results were
unsatisfactory, the candidate was not considered.
The focus of the assessment instruments was on the
specific skills needed for the first-line supervisor
position. Three exercises were used during a one and one-
half day session: an in-basket exercise, a production
scheduling problem, and an exercise testing interpersonal
skills. The assessors were trained line managers two
levels above first-level supervisors plus an industrial
relations representative.

Developmental Approach

As a developmental device for middle managers in the
parts division, the company identified six skill areas --
e.g., leadership, decision making, initiative -- needed by
district managers. All middle managers went through this
assessment center.

==

The developmental assessment covered three days: the first half of the session involved exercises, while the second half was devoted to group experiences such as reality checking, needs determination, and developmental plans outlined by peers and assessors. The assessors of this group were for the most part district managers, generally two levels above those being assessed.

On the basis of identified strengths and areas to be improved, a developmental plan was devised for all middle managers. The atmosphere of this center was supportive and the outcomes were considered favorable by the company, assessors, and candidates.

APPENDIX

Discussion Questions and Issues

1. A company used a "packaged" assessment center with standardized assessment items and methods that was purchased from a consulting firm. Many managers felt that results weren't much better than "the old way" to do it. What's your reaction to this?

2. A firm in the sales field runs an assessment center regularly. It uses one item in the communications area. What are your thoughts regarding this practice and possible problems they might encounter?

3. Exhibit 7-1 provides a group of 17 different job dimensions thought to be important in this company. When this material was being developed, one of the senior managers remarked: "Don't know why we need all of those items and the time it'll take to get information on them. I've got a rule of thumb involving five managerial areas that give me all the information I need." How might you respond to this manager?

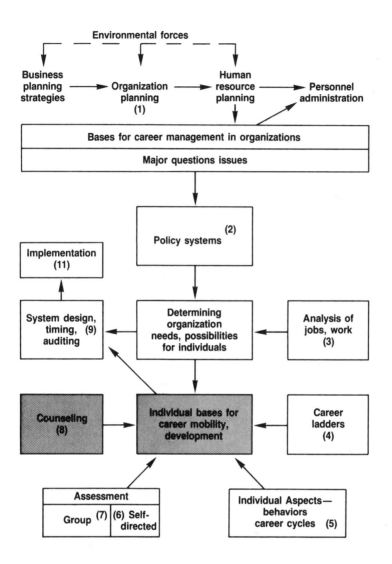

Environmental forces

Business planning strategies → Organization planning (1) → Human resource planning → Personnel administration

Bases for career management in organizations

Major questions issues

Policy systems (2)

Implementation (11)

System design, timing, (9) auditing

Determining organization needs, possibilities for individuals

Analysis of jobs, work (3)

Counseling (8)

Individual bases for career mobility, development

Career ladders (4)

Assessment

Group (7) | (6) Self-directed

Individual Aspects— behaviors career cycles (5)

Chapter Eight

Counseling and Career Pathing

CHAPTER EIGHT

CAREER COUNSELING

STAGES IN A CAREER COUNSELING SESSION

CAREER PATHING

APPENDIX

COUNSELING AND CAREER PATHING

CAREER COUNSELING

Counseling is basic to career planning, but such counseling takes place in many ways both within and outside the organization. Discussions with family, friends, colleagues, peers, as well as with professional psychologists, personnel counselors, and supervisors all influence an individual's career decisions. Easily the greatest counseling activity in the organization involves the supervisor and subordinate. Thus a formal session with a career counselor is a specialized event in what is otherwise a common situation.

Role of Personnel in Counseling

Counseling generally serves many different purposes: it provides sources of information; it permits the checking out of the counselee's ideas regarding plans for the future (reality checking); it serves as a sounding board to help the individual further shape and temper his or her own ideas; and it also serves to impart important, valid information on company opportunities, policies, and programs. Where counseling is part of a session with a professional, the results from various skill and attitudinal instruments may be discussed. Career counseling plays an important role in terms of the fulfillment of company human resource plans. Since CMO is concerned with assuring future staffing needs of the organization, career pathing and counseling serve a necessary function in meeting these objectives. In career-related counseling, for example, individuals find out about such things as:

===

* job requirements, duties, and responsibilities,

* skills and abilities to meet work demands,

* occupational structures,

* career ladders, and

* bases for personal development.

In addition, organizations can stay more in touch with their employees - learning of their abilities, needs, and desires - by formalizing counseling processes. The person providing the career counseling helps the organization member to design a personal "game plan" that reflects organizational requirements and future possibilities. Where counseling is a part of a particular target job, as in management development, career pathing is usually quite specific and includes timing for the accomplishment of steps involved.

Personnel's role is to support manager-employee relationships. This means they often assist line managers in the counseling process by supplying specific career data, explaining procedures for career pathing, and helping to establish training for supervisory roles in counseling.

Role of Line Managers in Counseling

Some of the most important individual counseling occurs informally by supervisors and line managers. Supervisors are good sources of job information and, more importantly, serve as "guides" to help an individual think through career issues. However, to be effective at such counseling, a line manager needs the appropriate skills, such as effective listening, empathy, and problem solving, as well as reliable information about careers in the organization. This is a major challenge in many organizations where supervisors and managers are not kept informed of these developments.

Some aspects of career counseling, both formal and informal, involve giving advice, though this is being de-

emphasized in favor of the individual taking more complete
charge of his or her career. Correspondingly, CMO tends
to de-emphasize advice giving, preferring instead to
stress reality checking of an individual's desires with
what's available in the organization. Even so, advice
will be asked for, and when it is, all those involved in
career counseling need to have a firm grasp of
organizational needs as well as a sense of an individual's
abilities and skills.

Career Counseling and Appraisal Interviews

        Traditional appraisals. Some companies include
career counseling as part of their traditional appraisal
interview. However, the two activities are entirely
different in focus, direction, and type of information
used.

    1. Career counseling focuses on individual career
        plans, whereas appraisal interviewing has a
        strong organizational focus, i.e., what the
        individual is doing for the benefit of the
        company.

    2. Career counseling helps an individual develop
        career paths by informing him or her of career
        ladders and job requirements; the traditional
        appraisal interview judges a person's past
        performance and compares this performance with
        established company standards.

    3. The results of career counseling to help a
        person set goals and a career program are
        contrary to traditional appraisals that affect
        promotion, transfer, or salary recommendations.

        However, there is a notable area of change affecting
appraisals that is resulting in driving it much closer to
the focus and approaches of career counseling.

        Developmental appraisals. Although traditional
appraisal interviews run counter to career counseling,

==

DEVELOPMENTAL PERFORMANCE APPRAISALS can be mutually supportive. Exhibit 8-1 outlines the features of a developmental appraisal. The focus of this type of appraisal is quite different from traditional approaches.

1. The developmental appraisal is structured to improve the two-way communication.

2. Individual development is stressed -- "what can be done to improve past performance?"

3. The appraisal is divided into two sessions: the first covering the performance issues and the second compiling a personal development and performance plan.

The emphasis in developmental appraisals is on establishing a better working relationship between supervisor and subordinate by improving communication and understanding.

STAGES IN A CAREER COUNSELING SESSION

Career counseling processes have been studied in order to develop more systematic and effective approaches. One model that has proven effective models the career counseling process in three stages, each of which has specific objectives and requires the use of certain skills. The success of each stage depends on how successfully the preceding stage has been accomplished. Regardless of whether the interview is formal or informal, the counseling supervisor is viewed as the "expert" and so should act in a way that engenders trust.

Stage 1: Opening Up and Probing

The first stage in the counseling process relies heavily on good communication skills. The individual needs to be put at ease so he or she will talk candidly to a supervisor. The rapport between them insures an honest discussion of values, goals, interests, and abilities,

EXHIBIT 8-1: Features of a Developmental Appraisal

1. Introduction

   - Atmosphere should be nonthreatening.
   - Two-way communication is important.
   - Individual does talking and states his or her view.

2. Individual's view

   - Assesses job performance.
   - Comments on working climate.
   - Discusses opportunities for career advancement.
   - Makes suggestions for change and improvement.

3. Supervisor's view

   - Issues summary statement.
   - Emphasizes critical skills and abilities (no more than three).
   - Avoids comparisons with others.
   - Begins with strengths.
   - Mentions major weaknesses only as opportunities for improvement.

4. Performance plan

   - Should be employee's plan.
   - Includes counseling and advising by supervisor.
   - Includes timetable.
   - Has concurrence of supervisor.

5. Personal development plan

   - Points out future advancement possibilities, given adequate or good performance.
   - Includes frank discussion of organizational response to marginal or poor performance.
   - Emphasizes skills needed and how to improve them.
   - Includes timetable.

6. Conclusion

   - Supervisor asks for questions and additional concerns.
   - Closes on positive note.

SOURCE: Adapted from Elmer H. Burack and Nicholas J. Mathys, Career Management in Organizations: A Practical Human Resource Planning Approach (Lake Forest, IL: Brace Park Press, 1980), p. 298.

==

thus leading to a clear picture of a career.

Usually by asking the right questions, a supervisor builds confidence in the employee and elicits necessary information and ideas. Two types of questions are appropriate for counseling purposes: open-ended ones to help a person loosen up, and probing questions to specify issues, clarify information, and examine assumptions. For example, open-ended questions most often begin discussions -- e.g., "What seems to be the matter?" -- whereas probing questions explore deeper or specific sources of discontent -- e.g., "Is there anything specific about your job that needs improving?" Exhibit 8-2 shows a sample of informal counseling that exemplifies the three stages in a session.

A supervisor as counselor also needs to cultivate listening skills. In addition to the spoken word, effective listening involves attention to nonverbal messages carried by tone of voice, body language, and other physical signals. Steady eye contact and an occasional nod of the head can let the employee know he or she is understood and being taken seriously.

Moreover, empathy, the ability to participate in the feelings or ideas of another, is a prerequisite for all counseling. If a supervisor can empathize with subordinates, then he or she can come up with appropriate questions and be attentive to their needs and desires. (Specific exercises for developing skills needed for this and the other two stages are included in Chapter 5 of Burack and Mathys, Career Management in Organizations.)

Stage 2:   Understanding and Focusing

As stage 1 emphasizes understanding an individual's experience, stage 2 shifts to a more objective perspective and helps people see themselves in relation to the alternatives available. Specific issues and problems must be identified and dealt with. A supervisor at this stage may have to get more career information on career ladders, organizational needs in the future, etc. from the personnel department.

As a result of both experience and access to valid information, a supervisor can provide necessary reality checking of an employee's career ideas and lead him or her

EXHIBIT 8-2:   Scenario of a Counseling Interview

John Bannon, a college graduate, has been working for Wilson Press as a
production scheduler for the past three years. He had a good work record
until recently, when his performance sharply declined. His supervisor
decided that a frank discussion was in order regarding his performance and
general attitude.

STAGE 1: OPENING UP AND PROBING

SUP: Oh, Hi, John! Come on in   Supervisor sets up a relaxed, non-
and have a seat.   threatening atmosphere.

JOHN: Don't mind if I do. (Looking
a little nervous.)

SUP: John, since you've come here   Supervisor begins with open-ended
you've been one of my best workers.   questions to encourage employee to
Lately, though, I've noticed a drop in   talk frankly.
your performance, which is unusual for
you. What seems to be the matter?

JOHN: Well, I don't really know--it
just seems that things are the same
day after day. Maybe I've just got
the blahs.

SUP: Maybe you feel bored and I can   Supervisor empathizes with employee
understand that; we all do at times.   and shows respect for his feelings.

JOHN: Well--it's not just that. I
thought if I got a college education
and worked hard, I'd be promoted.
I've been here three years and not
much has been happening.

SUP: I can appreciate your feelings;   Empathy is tempered with reality
hard work and good performance should   checking. Supervisor asks probing
be rewarded, but sometimes it takes   question.
longer than expected. Lately there
have been few position openings, which
is something neither of us has much
control over. Let's try to work on
what we can control! Is there anything
specific about your job that needs
improvement or that I can help you with?

EXHIBIT 8-2: Scenario of a Counseling Interivew (cont'd)

JOHN: Well--yes. I've pretty much got things down to a routine, but sometimes it's difficult to convince some of the department heads to follow the schedule.

. . . and gets specific complaint.

SUP: John, this is an area that we need to discuss further. Let's agree to get together tomorrow, say around four o'clock when things slow down so we can talk some more. OK?

Supervisor realizes she needs more information. Arranges for a time convenient with employee for further counseling.

JOHN: Gee, I'm taking a class. Can we make it Thursday?

SUP: No problem--please stop by at about four and we can continue.

In the intervening time, the supervisor contacts the personnel office and gets job-career information appropriate for John's case. It turns out to be complete and helpful regarding career ladders, needs, and general future requirements. John and the supervisor meet again on Thursday. The supervisor briefly recaps their previous discussion and the area they started to focus on.

STAGE 2: UNDERSTANDING AND FOCUSING

SUP: It seems to me then that persuasion is an area you need to work on. It's likely that other jobs at Wilson Press will require the ability to influence others concerning your own ideas. It seems to me that working on this area is likely to be beneficial for future jobs when openings do come up. Does that make sense to you?

Supervisor points out skill areas to develop that affect employee's immediate performance and his long-run career possibilities.

JOHN: Yes, I never thought about it like that before.

Employee begins to see larger picture of organization alternatives.

SUP: Why don't you think about other areas of your job that also might be improved? I'd be really interested in seeing what you come up with.

EXHIBIT 8-2: Scenario of a Counseling Interivew (cont'd)

JOHN: Yes, I think I'd enjoy that.

SUP: Tell me, John, do you feel that you're ready for promotion?

Once trust is established supervisor can ask another probing (direct) question,

JOHN: Yes.

SUP: Did you have particular types of work or any special positions in mind?

. . . followed by another,

JOHN: Well--yes, I thought I might be ready for a line supervisor's job or the production planner's job.

. . . to focus career objectives.

SUP: Those are quite different kinds of jobs. Are there any particular reasons you are considering them?

Supervisor provides reality checking and points out areas of conflict.

JOHN: Not really. I just think they're good jobs.

The supervisor describes the job and responsibilities of line supervisors at length. She also takes out a recently updated job description, and she and John analyze it point by point. The supervisor also calls over an employee recently promoted to this type of position, who further describes details of the job to John. The line supervisor has to leave, but John and the supervisor resume the discussion and also talk about the production planner's job.

STAGE 3: PROGRAMMING

SUP: When we were talking before, John, you mentioned that you felt both the line supervisor and production planner jobs were good ones. You're right. I feel they are, too. Let's work out a plan that will hopefully meet both your needs and the company's. How about thinking over what parts of your job you like most and which you like least and compare that with the foreman's job and the planner's job? Also, why not think about other skills related to these jobs that maybe you haven't had a chance to use?

Supervisor starts employee working on an action plan and a review of his skills.

EXHIBIT 8-2: Scenario of a Counseling Interivew (cont'd)

JOHN: That makes sense.

SUP: Also, you can check with personnel to get the actual requirements of those jobs. They have a pretty extensive career file. Also, it's important to recognize that you happen to have picked out two jobs that have high priority for future needs. Naturally, it'll be a competitive situation; but at least you're looking at jobs with good growth potential and that will be growing in numbers.

Supervisor guides employee to other sources of information. She also remains supportive, but realistic about career possibilities.

JOHN: Okay.

SUP: Since your appraisal review is coming up in two weeks we can discuss what you find out then. Hopefully, we can develop a specific plan that will meet your needs.

Supervisor sets up a future time so she and employee can devise a development plan.

JOHN: I hope so, too. You've given me a lot to think about and by then I'll have had time to sort things through.

Employee has better sense of his career possibilities and so can better take charge.

SUP: Remember, I'm available for help if you need it.

JOHN: Thanks. This has helped me a lot.

SOURCE: Adapted from information in Gerard Egan, The Skilled Helper (Monterrey, CA: Brooks/Cole Publishing, 1975).

==

to consider areas of potential conflict between career and life goals or between goals and current skills. It is important at this stage for a supervisor to avoid stereotyping jobs and employees by sex or race. Also, a counseling supervisor should not force his or her values on an employee, but concentrate on what is right for a particular individual.

Stage 3: Programming

A career program resulting from the counseling process usually is characterized by realistic career choices and detailed action steps. Information from work analyses as well as career ladders is invaluable in charting an individual's career path. The important counseling skill for this stage is problem solving.

CAREER PATHING

Career pathing represents the last stage in the series of individually oriented activities: needs analysis, assessment, counseling, and career pathing. Before compiling career paths, the individual must either have developed his or her career goals and objectives or have become formally involved in organizational plans for future staffing.

Career Path Worksheet

The form for a career path worksheet is varied and informal. Exhibit 8-3 shows one such worksheet for Linda Robinson, a high school teacher who changed careers to become Personnel Development Specialist for a houseware manufacturing and distribution firm. Ms. Robinson's career paths reflect the amount of retraining that was necessary through in-house supervisory courses, a tuition-assistance program, and several management workshops. It also shows future paths and alternatives in her career progression.

EXHIBIT 8-3: Career Path Worksheet: Linda Robinson

	Previous	-5	-4	-3	-2	-1	Today	1	2	3	4	5
Jobs		• Student	• Teacher			• Development specialist		Path 1: Development supr.		Asst. pers. mgr.		Pers. mgr. ?
								Path 2:	Trng. coordinator		Asst. dir. of trng.	?
Formal education	B.S. + M.A. (Math) (English)			Acct I Acct II		Personnel Development		Path 1 Personnel Management I		Personnel Management II	Personnel Seminar	
Training and development				Super. Training	Management Workshop			Path 1		None?	Management Workshop II	
								Path 2				
Other (indicate)	Outside Training courses			A.B.A. program	AMA commun.			Path 1		None?		U. of Mich
								Path 2		NTL		
Experience, skills, etc. acquired			Dealing with people and co-workers	Problem analysis Developing schedules Needs to develop people		Needs analysis	Job description	Job analysis Path 1 Development and Programming	Training media	Conduct training programs	Planning	Managing HR / Design of purchase programs
								Path 2				
Previous	1977	1978	1979	1980	1981	Today 1982	1983	1984	1985	1986	1987	

SOURCE: Adapted from Elmer H. Burack and Nicholas J. Mathys, Career Management Organizations: A Practical Human Resource Planning Approach (Lake Forest, IL: Brace Park Press, 1980), p. 329.

===

Whatever the form of a career path worksheet, the following items need to be included.

* General representations of specific activities and times.

* Both past and future events.

* Work and nonwork activities, i.e., job experiences, training, education, professional/ community activities, even hobbies.

* Alternative career paths to allow for speculation and flexibility.

Reviewing Past Experience

A proper interpretation of past experience in determining career direction is as important as identifying skills, only some of which may be known. In fact, careful analysis of past experiences may uncover skills not realized before. The individual, with the guidance of the counselor, should take a look behind specific training courses or academic degrees to discover the enduring abilities or insights. For instance, a person who took a computer programming course several years ago may not have the skills for today's changing technology. However, this same person may have learned a system of thinking and approach to problem analysis that is valuable and relevant. Especially for those (mostly women) who reenter the work force, current abilities and skills can be culled from past experiences, say in community organizations (organizing, planning) teaching (administrative, leadership), or even housework (planning, budgeting).

APPENDIX

Discussion Questions and Issues

1. Some personnel people question whether line managers
    can be objective in a career counseling role with
    subordinates, especially if it might result in the
    loss of a valued department member. What is your
    opinion?

2. What practical problems need to be dealt with in the
    organization's or manager's response to poor
    performance?

3. What difficulties is an organization likely to face
    that attempts to shift its traditional appraisal
    system to one that increasingly emphasizes the
    developmental aspects?

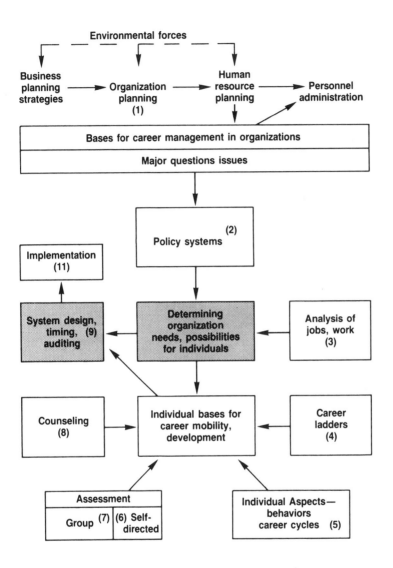

Environmental forces

```
Business          Human
planning  ──▶  Organization  ──▶  resource  ──▶  Personnel
strategies     planning         planning        administration
               (1)
```

| Bases for career management in organizations |
| Major questions issues |

Policy systems (2)

Implementation (11)

System design, timing, (9) auditing

Determining organization needs, possibilities for individuals

Analysis of jobs, work (3)

Counseling (8)

Individual bases for career mobility, development

Career ladders (4)

| Assessment | |
| Group (7) | (6) Self-directed |

Individual Aspects— behaviors career cycles (5)

Chapter Nine

Auditing and Initiating a Career Planning System

CHAPTER NINE

AUDITING THE CAREER PLANNING SYSTEM

Format

Procedure for Scoring

Step 1

Step 2

Step 3

Step 4

Audit Analyses - Application Example

CP Audit as Performance Standards

INITIATING A CAREER PROGRAM

Setting Time Schedules

Examples of Time Schedules

CASE APPLICATION OF A CAREER PROGRAM

Exhibit 9-1: The Career Planning Audit

Exhibit 9-2: Analysis of Time Priorities

APPENDIX

Discussion Questions and Issues

AUDITING AND INITIATING A CAREER PLANNING SYSTEM

AUDITING THE CAREER PLANNING SYSTEM

Format

A format for auditing the career planning system which we have found helpful includes 13 major categories and 52 activities commonly associated with CMO programs. The format as presented in Exhibit 9-1 has a two-fold purpose:

*   to establish the organization's current status as to activities associated with CMO, and

*   to identify future possibilities for a more comprehensive system.

Procedure for Scoring

The procedure for scoring the audit is made up of four steps.

Step 1. Score all 52 items in the 13 categories under the column "current state of activity;" this appraisal represents the organization's current status as to activities associated with CMO.

Step 2. For all 52 items, and under the column headed "current need," put a check beside the ones that represent the current need of CP, i.e., today or within the immediate future.

Step 3. Represents the calculations for current opportunities. The current opportunity score represents the difference between your "current possibilities" and the "current situation" on CMO-related items. First

EXHIBIT 9-1: The Career Planning Audit

0	1	2	3	4	5	6	7	8	9	10

Little or no work done in this area.

Some work underway; loosely organized; informal relationships.

Organized activity; part of regular system; formal relationships.

Major progress and improvements; starting to validate activity.

Advanced state; infused into line management; flexible and adaptive to new needs.

Areas of human resource planning	Current state of activity	Current need (✓)
1. Work (job) analysis		
.job description accurate, complete (traditional)	0 1 2 3 4 5 6 7 8 9 10	_____
.required end behaviors	0 1 2 3 4 5 6 7 8 9 10	_____
.identification, job families	0 1 2 3 4 5 6 7 8 9 10	_____
.career ladders	0 1 2 3 4 5 6 7 8 9 10	_____
2. Transfer, promotion		
.policy developed	0 1 2 3 4 5 6 7 8 9 10	_____
.top management involvement	0 1 2 3 4 5 6 7 8 9 10	_____
.development uses	0 1 2 3 4 5 6 7 8 9 10	_____
.choices shared with employee	0 1 2 3 4 5 6 7 8 9 10	_____
3. Succession planning		
.policy developed	0 1 2 3 4 5 6 7 8 9 10	_____
.key positions identified	0 1 2 3 4 5 6 7 8 9 10	_____
.succession ladders created	0 1 2 3 4 5 6 7 8 9 10	_____
.vulnerability analysis (backup) developed	0 1 2 3 4 5 6 7 8 9 10	_____
.needs analysis for development of people	0 1 2 3 4 5 6 7 8 9 10	_____
4. Policy		
.promotion, transfer, hiring	0 1 2 3 4 5 6 7 8 9 10	_____
.budget support, CP programs	0 1 2 3 4 5 6 7 8 9 10	_____
.systems emphasis	0 1 2 3 4 5 6 7 8 9 10	_____
.integration into business planning and human resource planning	0 1 2 3 4 5 6 7 8 9 10	_____
5. Employee file information		
.personnel data base	0 1 2 3 4 5 6 7 8 9 10	_____
.performance data	0 1 2 3 4 5 6 7 8 9 10	_____
.behavioral, assessment data	0 1 2 3 4 5 6 7 8 9 10	_____
.system update, capability	0 1 2 3 4 5 6 7 8 9 10	_____
.retrieval capability	0 1 2 3 4 5 6 7 8 9 10	_____
6. Career paths		
.identification of movement patterns	0 1 2 3 4 5 6 7 8 9 10	_____
.developmental positions identified	0 1 2 3 4 5 6 7 8 9 10	_____
.lateral movements	0 1 2 3 4 5 6 7 8 9 10	_____

EXHIBIT 9-1: The Career Planning Audit (cont'd)

Areas of human resource planning	Current state of activity	Current need (√)
7. Communication--available jobs		
.line management involvement	0 1 2 3 4 5 6 7 8 9 10	_____
.job posting	0 1 2 3 4 5 6 7 8 9 10	_____
.priority rules established	0 1 2 3 4 5 6 7 8 9 10	_____
8. Counseling		
.use of trained line managers	0 1 2 3 4 5 6 7 8 9 10	_____
.specialists available	0 1 2 3 4 5 6 7 8 9 10	_____
.outcounseling program	0 1 2 3 4 5 6 7 8 9 10	_____
.self-assessment program	0 1 2 3 4 5 6 7 8 9 10	_____
9. Personnel development		
.knowledge of job characteristics	0 1 2 3 4 5 6 7 8 9 10	_____
.individual needs analysis	0 1 2 3 4 5 6 7 8 9 10	_____
.tuition remibursement program	0 1 2 3 4 5 6 7 8 9 10	_____
.development positions, strategies	0 1 2 3 4 5 6 7 8 9 10	_____
.high potential program	0 1 2 3 4 5 6 7 8 9 10	_____
.in-house training and development programs	0 1 2 3 4 5 6 7 8 9 10	_____
10. Career-related information		
.typical paths communicated	0 1 2 3 4 5 6 7 8 9 10	_____
.organizational opportunity shared with employee	0 1 2 3 4 5 6 7 8 9 10	_____
.position pay ranges	0 1 2 3 4 5 6 7 8 9 10	_____
11. Retirement planning		
.formal policy	0 1 2 3 4 5 6 7 8 9 10	_____
.counseling availability	0 1 2 3 4 5 6 7 8 9 10	_____
.formal programs	0 1 2 3 4 5 6 7 8 9 10	_____
12. Performance appraisal		
.agreed-on job needs	0 1 2 3 4 5 6 7 8 9 10	_____
.performance standards	0 1 2 3 4 5 6 7 8 9 10	_____
.developmental system	0 1 2 3 4 5 6 7 8 9 10	_____
.validity analyses	0 1 2 3 4 5 6 7 8 9 10	_____
13. Assessment of potential (beyond appraisal information)		
.individual/group approaches	0 1 2 3 4 5 6 7 8 9 10	_____
.validity analyses	0 1 2 3 4 5 6 7 8 9 10	_____
.counseling	0 1 2 3 4 5 6 7 8 9 10	_____
.career pathing	0 1 2 3 4 5 6 7 8 9 10	_____

SOURCE: Reprinted with permission from Elmer H. Burack and Nicholas J. Mathys, Career Management in Organizations: A Practical Human Resource Planning Approach (Lake Forest, IL: Brace Park Press, 1980), pp. 333-335.

calculate a score for current possibilities by totalling the number of items you checked as "current need" times the maximum number of points for each (10). In other words, the current possibilities score represents the highest score (10 points) for the items you checked as "current need." If your current possibilities score is 520 points, that would mean you have checked all the items as "current need." Your current possibilities score could not exceed 520 points, which is the total number of current need items times ten. Next, figure the current situation score by totalling the scores only for those items checked off as current need.

Your current opportunity score equals the difference between current possibilities and current situation.

$$\frac{\text{current}}{\text{opportunity}} = \frac{\text{current}}{\text{possibilities}} - \frac{\text{current}}{\text{situation}}$$

To simplify interpretation, calculate current opportunity as a percentage, i.e., current situation divided by current possibilities times 100%.

$$\frac{\text{current}}{\text{opportunity}}^{(\%)} = \frac{\text{current situation}}{\text{current possibilities}} \times 100\%$$

Common interpretations attached to the current opportunity (%) suggest that ratings above 80% indicate good realization of possibilities for the company's "current situations."

Step 4. To calculate a future potential score for CMO, total all of the scored items (current state) and subtract the total from 520 (maximum score for CMO). This is only one indicator of future potential but it does provide a base line for future planning. Each company must establish for itself the scope and specifics of its future program and the time span that can best accommodate these.

==

Audit Analyses - Application Example

The following company situation is typical of those found using the HR audit approach. A medium-sized sales-service organization undertook a career planning program three years prior to the audit. The Director of Management Development and Career Planning checked 40 different items (of the 52) as current need. The point total for those 40 items was 240 points. This analysis provided the basis for the following calculations.

Current possibilities: 40 x 10 = 400 points

Current situation: (for the 40 items)   240 points

Current opportunity (points):   400-240 = 160 points

Current opportunity (percent): $\frac{240}{400}$ x 100% = 60%

Interpretation: On the basis of the 60% penetration (current opportunity) considerable refinement of the current system was possible.

The Director also carried out the calculations for future possibilities.

Maximum possible: 520 points

Current situation: 240 points

Future possibilities (points): 520-240 = 280 points

Future possibilities (percent): $\frac{240}{520}$ x 100% = 46%

Interpretation: In terms of longer-run system development, only about one-half of the future possibilities had been realized at the time of the audit.

==

The set of calculations for "current opportunity" and
"future possibilities" provided two base lines for judging
the current state of system development and areas that
could be considered for the future. The Director then
started to look much more closely at specific item scores
in the light of current problems, issues, and future
plans. This more intensive item analysis set the stage
for prioritizing future directions for systems
development. For example, the "current situation" for the
40 items checked as "current need" was 240 points, an
average of 6 points per item. Given the fact that the
system was only three years old at the time of analysis,
the score for "current situation" suggested quite good
progress. However, under the work analysis category, the
Director noted that the traditional job descriptions were
rated at "8" while "required end behaviors" were rated at
"1." If future progress was to be made in facilitating
internal promotions of women out of employee ranks into
supervision, much better information was needed regarding
targeted jobs. Providing a detailed set of job
responsibilities to a person analyzing her career
possibilities was of little real help in understanding the
dynamics and work requirements of a particular position.
The item "required end behaviors" received much attention
in future systems development.

CP Audit as Performance Standards

Personnel officials and career planners, like their
peers in marketing, finance, and production, are
increasingly looking at programs in terms of costs and
benefits as a basis for launching results-oriented
activities. Yet it is sometimes difficult to evaluate
program elements of career planning where benefits are
often intangible and not easy to measure.

The career planning audit offers one way to quantify
career programs. The 13 areas of audit provide a basis
for establishing performance standard by which activities
and results can be judged. The list, though hardly
exhaustive, can help officials determine whether new
policies are achieving the intended results in a timely
way. For example, if a company institutes a program to

improve career mobility, one measure of its impact would be the increase in the number of lateral transfers compared to those in the past. The "lateral movements" item under category 6, "career paths," would provide the basis for a careful study of this factor.

Tracking performance measured over time serves several purposes:

* It lets personnel officials know what to expect as "normal" performance so they can set realistic program targets.

* It indicates the extent to which line managers and supervisors have cooperated in facilitating the launching of newer career-related activities.

* It provides data for action research.

* It can help uncover relationships between career statistics and general business performance.

* It can provide a basis for studying the relationships between career statistics and absenteeism and turnover.

INITIATING A CAREER PROGRAM

Setting Time Schedules

The time schedule of a career program depends on many variables: enterprise needs, business objectives, and general priorities; overall economic size of the organization; physical dispersion of units; the variety of employee groups to be included; the organization's future needs and strategies; and the current state of planning and career systems development. In short, no "typical" time estimate exists. However, there are some common conditions to consider when estimating time for a systems installation:

1. Perhaps the only constant of tentative time frames for career programs is that most time

==

estimates are overly optimistic. This is
especially true of programs that depart
significantly from previous activities. It is
not uncommon for time estimates to be off by a
factor of 2 or 3 where analyses are done
"loosely."

2.   The limited number of people or other resources
available for assignment to the program must
also be considered in a workable time estimate.

3.   Organization or business problems will appear so
that a specific career program may have to be
set aside temporarily -- no matter how desirable
it may be to continue working on it.

4.   Many activities must take place sequentially.
It's not realistic to discuss individual career
plans for example, unless people know what the
job involves.

Examples of Time Schedules

The following company experiences may help to judge
some of the time requirements of career planning.

In a small insurance company of 3000 employees, the
time requirement for installing a basic career program was
about 18 months. The program included (1) an update of
job descriptions and structures, and (2) a review and
extension of career ladder information. Most of the
responsibility for program planning fell to one person.
Clear limits also existed as to how fast various phases
could be undertaken.

In a large organization employing some 15,000 people,
the career program was an extension of existing human
resource planning. Their program consisted of (1) the
updating of job descriptions and specifications, (2)
enlarging the base of individual knowledge, performance,
and skill data, (3) the development of employee career
workshops. The addition of two planners to the corporate
staff was necessary in order to accomplish the design and
launch the activities. The program required two years.
Because of the extended time period, the managers of

personnel, human resources, and career planning worked
closely together and with line managers to redirect the
activities as circumstances warranted.

CASE APPLICATION OF A CAREER PROGRAM

Martin National Bank, a large conservative bank
located in the east, employed over 6,000 people. The bank
was organized along traditional lines, with strength and
much responsibility centered in major departments. In
total, nine department heads reported to the president's
office.
Martin's management faced a difficult task as it
prepared to cope with a rapidly changing environment.
Both on the domestic and international fronts, changes in
social, legal, and economic conditions called for a
different type of management approach. In addition to
traditional managers, Martin National needed flexible and
growth-oriented managers who could initiate change.
Two situations led to the need for further management
development and employee training:

* Business growth and diversification
  necessitated a larger pool of managerial talent
  that could be channeled into these activities.

* The clerical group considered the bank seriously
  deficient in "opportunity" for movement into
  management.

Consequently, a project team consisting of key
section heads was formed to investigate these issues and
set priorities. This was a critical step before any
meaningful career activity could take place. The study
team focused on 19 major employee groupings around three
skill levels: low and entry level, intermediate level,
and high-skill level. While it was not clear initially
what programs might be recommended to top management, the
Vice President of Personnel helped to establish ground
rules:

1. All plans for corrective action would have to
   fit into general organizational plans.

2.   Resources were available for only a limited
     number of new(er) activities.

3.   Long-term growth needs of the bank had to be
     considered along with the short-term pressures.

By means of an impact analysis,[**] the study team
identified the thrust the CP activities had on various
problem areas. The need areas highlighted by the analysis
were as follows:

*   Accurate work analyses to ensure detailed job
     descriptions.

*   Communication of job availability, the major
     components of which are counseling,
     identification of career paths, job posting, and
     managerial support for employees.

*   Employee development and career planning by
     identifying job families and career ladders as
     well as supplying information on careers and
     means of qualifying for them.

*   New policies for facilitating promotions,
     transfers, and lateral movements.

*   Individual needs analysis to determine what
     skills and training an employee needed for a
     job.

*   A functional performance appraisal system for
     assuring good standards and informing employees
     about their future job possibilities.

This impact analysis helped in setting time
priorities for the overall human resource planning system
(see Exhibit 9-2) and the sequence[**] of the CP program as
well.

[**]See Exhibit 10-1 for the form of an impact analysis
and Exhibit 10-2 for the planning sequence form.

EXHIBIT 9-2: Analysis of Time Priorities

CAREER ISSUES AND PROBLEMS	TIME PRIORITY	SYSTEM ELEMENTS	TIME PRIORITY
Shortages: officers/managers	●●●	Job analysis	●●●
Career mobility, employees	●	Transfer, promotion	●
EEO: women/low skill areas	●●●	Succession planning	●
Availability: job information	●●●	Policy	●●
Employee training	●	Employee file information	●
Turnover--management		Career paths	●●●
trainees	●●	Communication--	
Shift: EEO monitoring agency	--	job availability	●●●
Link: corporate and HR plans	●	Counseling	●●●
Inability to transfer people	●	Personnel development	●
Top management commitment to HR	●●	Career-related information	●●
Lack of workable job			
information skills	●●●	Retirement	●
Employee knowledge of career			
paths	●●		
Supervisory knowledge--			
available jobs	●●●		
Supervisory counseling and			
training	●●●		
Posting and timing, accuracy	●●		
Release of good performers:			
senior managers	●		
Performance standards	●●●		
Identify high-potential			
employees	●		
Mobility of specialists	●	Time priorities: ●●● = within 9 months	
Conflict resolution: succession	●●	●● = 10-18 months	
Managerial rewards--HR support	●●	● = 19-24 months	

SOURCE: Reprinted with permission from Elmer H. Burack and Nicholas J. Mathys,
Career Management in Organizations: A Practical Human Resource Planning Approach
(Lake Forest IL: Brace Park Press, 1980), p. 354.

===

Any organization will encounter problems during
installation of a career program. For Martin National
Bank, the problems centered around performance appraisals
and job postings.

The performance appraisal system was often
inconsistently applied throughout the organization, and in
many cases good performance standards were lacking. To
remedy this deficiency, Martin tied the activity more
closely to other system components, namely complete job
descriptions and individual assessments. In this way the
importance of an appraisal system for promotion decisions
and assessing individual potential was emphasized.

Like the appraisal system, the job posting system was
unevenly administered. In addition, there was often a
lack of reliable job information, and the effort itself
never received top management support. More detailed
policies setting priorities for the treatment of
candidates plus an improved appraisal system helped to
offset these problems.

===

APPENDIX

Discussion Questions and Issues

1.   The Personnel Department of a firm audited its career
      planning system and related support activities. The
      "audit" score was quite high overall, but very low
      scores were indicated on categories 8 (Counseling)
      and 13 (Assessment of potential). How would you
      react to these results?

2.   A company had used the "audit" approach for three
      years and noted that in at least one category, Career
      ladders (No. 6), scores actually worsened. What
      implications might you infer from these results?

3.   A company audit of its HR system indicated a very low
      score on the item "use of trained line managers"
      (category 8, Counseling). When this was reviewed
      with senior line managers, they told HR officials
      that "this was not their responsibility and further,
      they had little time to do this in any type of
      complete way." What approaches might be indicated in
      dealing with this situation?

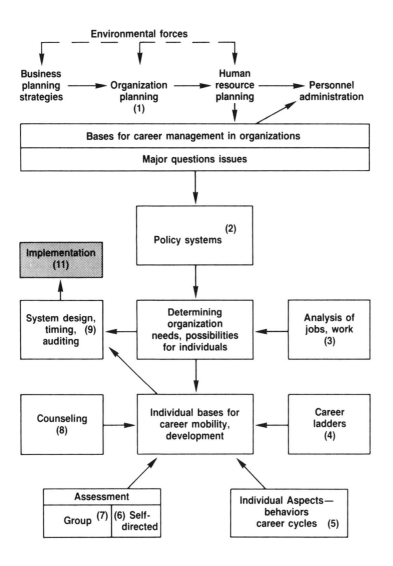

Environmental forces

Business planning strategies → Organization planning (1) → Human resource planning → Personnel administration

Bases for career management in organizations

Major questions issues

Policy systems (2)

Implementation (11)

System design, timing, auditing (9) ← Determining organization needs, possibilities for individuals ← Analysis of jobs, work (3)

Counseling (8) → Individual bases for career mobility, development ← Career ladders (4)

Assessment

Group (7) | (6) Self-directed

Individual Aspects—behaviors career cycles (5)

Chapter Ten

Instituting a Career Planning System

CHAPTER TEN

ANDERSON AND MASON: A CASE STUDY OF CAREER MANAGEMENT

    Structure and Problems

    Action Research

    Impact Analysis and Setting Priorities

    Long-Term Changes

CONCLUDING REMARKS

Exhibit 10-1: Impact Analysis for Anderson and Mason

Exhibit 10-2: Time Sequence of a Career Planning System
                for Anderson and Mason

APPENDIX

    Discussion Questions and Issues

INSTITUTING A CAREER PLANNING SYSTEM

ANDERSON AND MASON: A CASE STUDY OF CAREER MANAGEMENT

The following case study highlights and exemplifies some elements of CMO discussed in this book.[*] Because of space limitations in this summary and the comprehensive nature of the systems analysis, design, and programming, we have chosen to discuss representative features of the CMO approach. These include action research for focusing issues, impact analysis to clarify problems and set priorities, planning of activities and time phasing, and a retrospective section covering the installation.

Structure and Problems

Anderson and Mason is an architectural firm organized as a partnership of three senior and twenty junior partners. The partners are responsible for overseeing a number of projects based on their areas of expertise. Before a CP program was instituted, the personnel department consisted of two people who concerned themselves primarily with benefits programs, hiring staff, and other house-keeping activities. Because the firm prided itself on promotion from within, most external hiring was for entry-level positions. Employee training and selection fell almost exclusively to senior architects and project managers, with personnel acting in only an administrative role.

147

---

[*]This case study, like other ones presented in this summary, is intended for purposes of illustration, analysis, and discussion. The viewpoints expressed here are not necessarily those of the management involved.

Despite a good benefit plan, the firm heard the grumblings of discontent from several areas:

1.   The most disruptive development was that the technicians, architects, and engineers wanted a union.

2.   The clerical staff was resentful.

3.   There was an increase in turnover among young architects and other talented technical people.

4.   Older staff and senior managers were having difficulty keeping up with new technological advances that were being integrated into project designs and the utilization of the computer in support of design, project management, and administrative planning.

Action Research

A human resource consulting group was brought in to uncover reasons for the problems and to suggest programs for overcoming them. The initial phase of their action research involved some 40 interviews of people selected from all departments. A second round of interviews was conducted among some 150 additional people. (In all about one-fourth of the firm was interviewed), and questionnaires were distributed to all organization members.

This action-oriented study revealed a widespread dissatisfaction among employees with existing policies and numerous organizational practices. Specific and key problems that emerged were as follows:

1.   Career mobility was very poor in the company:

      a.   women (all secretarial staff) and minorities were almost totally ignored,

      b.   lateral movement was nonexistent, and

==

c. information on job opportunities was informal at best and generally lacking.

2. Little communication and coordination took place between departments, even between partners.

3. Lack of challenge in jobs and promotion opportunities contributed to high turnover among young architects.

4. There was little managerial support of transfers and career growth.

5. Middle managers saw some of their skills becoming increasingly obsolete in work with computers, managerial techniques, and new material technology.

6. Performance standards were inconsistent in performance appraisals and assessing potential.

7. Job descriptions were outdated, even nonexistent for some jobs.

8. Career information about skills, abilities, and future needs was sketchy.

Two examples suggest the range of career-related problem uncovered in the study. One of the problems faced by this firm concerned the executive secretaries, all of whom were women. After many years of working closely with their secretaries, the partners discovered that they were unaware of their secretaries' business potential -- that in some cases the secretaries possessed the skills and qualifications required of managers. The fact that these women had been ignored raised the question of how many others in the firm had been similarly overlooked. Another example concerned project management involving architectural and engineering personnel. The study revealed that no guidelines existed as to how one could qualify for these jobs in terms of knowledge, skills, experience, and licenses. Additionally, project managers frequently lacked managerial skills (e.g., planning, cost-

==

controls, coordination) and people-related skills for assuming leadership and motivating project members.

Impact Analysis and Setting Priorities

The information from the interviews and questionnaire study provided the basis for crystallizing career issues and problems. Relating this information to activities commonly associated with CMO was the task of impact analysis. Exhibit 10-1 shows an impact analysis highlighting areas that must receive priority in a CP program. High-priority areas include:

* career mobility, especially for women, specialists, and minorities,

* availability of job and employee information,

* top management commitment to CP, and

* the need for accurate performance standards.

The row headings represent career issues and problems abstracted from the interview and questionnaire data. Column headings represent CMO components and activities. The impact rating (number of arrows) indicates the relative importance to the Anderson and Mason organization of the system feature (or lack thereof) for the career issue or problem area. Then, comparing the actual organizational capability against the need provided the basis for prioritizing activities and developing a time-phased plan.

Next, time priorities were set for the system components designed to deal with the career-related issues and problems. The method of display (Exhibit 10-2) is a Gantt-type chart that relates activities and timing. Note the initial stage, lasting one year, consisted of the survey plus the development of job analyses. These job analyses in turn provided the bases for establishing performance standards, formalizing a performance appraisal system, management development, and career pathing.

EXHIBIT 10-1: Impact Analysis for Anderson and Mason

System features

Career issues and problems	Job analysis	Transfer, promotion	Succession planning	Policy	Employee file information	Career paths	Communication of available jobs	Counseling	Personnel development	Career-related information	Retirement	Compensation	Assessment
Career mobility, employees, specialists	√√	√√√	√√	√√	√√√	√	√√	√√	√√	√√√	√√	√√√	√√√
EEO: women/low skill areas	√√√	√	√√√	√√√	√√√	√√√	√√√	√√	√√√	√√√	√	√	√√
Availability: job information	√√	√√	√	√	√	√√√	√√	√	√	√√√	√√√	√√√	
Employee training	√	√√	√√	√√	√√	√	√	√√√	√	√√	√√√	√√√	
Turnover--management trainees	√√√	√√	√	√	√√	√	√	√√√	√√√	√√	√√	√√√	
Technical obsolescence	√√	√√	√√	√√	√	√	√	√√√	√√√	√√	√	√√	
Link: corporate and HR plans	√√	√√	√√√	√√√	√√	√	√	√√	√√√	√√√	√		
Inability to transfer people	√√√	√√	√√√	√	√√	√	√	√√	√√√	√√	√		
Top management commitment to HR	√√√	√	√√√	√	√	√	√	√√	√√√	√√√	√	√	
Lack of workable job information skills	√√√	√	√	√√	√√	√	√√	√√	√√	√√√	√	√	√√
Employee knowledge of career paths	√	√	√	√	√√√	√√√	√√√	√√√	√	√√√	√	√√	√√
Supervisory knowledge of available jobs		√		√	√√	√√	√√	√	√	√√√	√√	√√	√√√
Supervisory counseling and training	√	√	√	√	√	√	√√√	√√√	√	√√	√		√
Posting: timing, accuracy	√	√√	√	√	√√√	√√√	√	√	√	√			
Release of good performers and senior management	√√√	√√√	√√	√√	√√	√√√	√√√	√	√	√√	√√	√√	
Performance standards	√√√	√	√	√√	√	√	√	√	√	√	√	√√√	√√
Identify high potential employees	√√√	√√	√√	√√	√	√	√	√√√	√√	√	√√√	√√√	√√√
Conflict resolution: succession	√√√	√√	√√√	√√√	√	√	√√√	√√√	√√	√√			
Managerial rewards for HR support	√√√	√√	√√√	√√√	√√√	√√√	√	√√	√√	√			√√√

Impact: √√√ = High √√ = Medium √ = Low

SOURCE: Reprinted with permission from Elmer H. Burack and Nicholas J. Mathys, Career Management in Organizations: A Practical Human Research Planning Approach (Lake Forest, IL: Brace Park Press, 1980), p. 391.

EXHIBIT 10-2: Time Sequence of a Career Planning System for Anderson and Mason

	Year #1	Year #2	Year #3	Year #4	Year #5
Planning		Feasibility	Link BP-HRP		
			Monitor and update		
			Career planning		
Administration		Job posting I Clerical-technical			Job posting II Managerial-professional
			Performance appraisal system		
		Phase I Develop forms, set priorities	Phase II Implement and monitor	Phase III Modify and update	
		Reward career development — Compensation system	Tie to performance appraisal		
		Training Partners, sr. mgrs., mgrs, sup.	Training Assessment center		
		Selection Internal high potential, women, minorities	Recruiting External EEO as guide		
Support	Consultant survey, job analysis				
			Personnel Management Information System		
		Individual needs	Integrate into BIS	Refine	
		Counseling	Career ladders Install		
		Identify paths			
		High potentials	Management development Professional-managerial	Update All personnel	
		Individual	Assessment Group for middle and project management		
		Action research			
		Satisfaction study—monitor and update yearly			

SOURCE: Reprinted with permission from Elmer H. Burack and Nicholas J. Mathys, Career Management in Organizations: A Practical Human Resource Planning Approach (Lake Forest, IL: Brace Park Press, 1980), p. 355.

Long-Term Changes

The CMO system that was eventually installed resulted in a major reorganization of Anderson and Mason's personnel practices. Some of the key activities were as follows:

1. Personnel information was integrated into a personnel management information system (PMIS) and then tied into existing business information and cost systems. Employee files were expanded to include information for performance in project assignments, performance appraisals and assessments of potential, personal knowledge and skill information, and the results of INDIVIDUAL NEEDS ANALYSIS.

2. Job descriptions were updated and detailed so that the requirements could be made available for individual development.

3. Policy was changed to encourage lateral transfers.

4. A position of career counselor was established by the firm, and an architect/engineer with project experience was assigned as a part-time counselor. This eventually became a rotating assignment that provided valuable experience for those carrying out these responsibilities.

5. Managers were trained in a series of sessions over a six-week period in procedures of performance appraisal. Other developmental activities included high-potential technical people who attended a Junior Management Development program for training in management techniques. Also, a company sabbatical program was started -- experienced managers were given leaves of absence to study new architectural technology and/or computers, then returned to conduct in-house seminars for others.

CONCLUDING REMARKS

Anderson and Mason had to undertake substantial changes of policy, procedure, and individual manager (partner) action to achieve the full benefit of CMO activities. This by no means is a model for CMO in other organizations. Limited resources have to be weighed against short- and long-term priorities -- without seriously interrupting business flow. For Anderson and Mason many special scheduling arrangements had to be made. Moreover, the active support of the partners made the program workable and gave it the kind of legitimacy such a multi-year effort demanded. And as the climate and circumstances began to change gradually, a credibility was affirmed between the firm and their employees that encouraged organization members to be patient for the future and supportive in the present.

===

APPENDIX

Discussion Questions and Issues

1. The first phase of the Anderson and Mason program
    involved an extensive action-research program to
    crystallize central problems and issues. How might
    this study and purposes have been made known to
    employees to avoid unreal expectations as to remedial
    actions?

2. The time activity plan (Exhibit 10-2) indicated about
    one year for the survey study and reworking of job
    analyses. If the Anderson and Mason partnership had
    wanted to launch some career-related activity at a
    point earlier than indicated by the plan, even if a
    symbolic gesture, what one might you have proposed
    and what were your major considerations?

3. One of the activities related to the CMO system was
    the preparation of department heads and project
    managers to do performance appraisals in expert and
    systematic fashion. What timing technique(s) would
    you propose to accomplish most effectively this phase
    of the program?

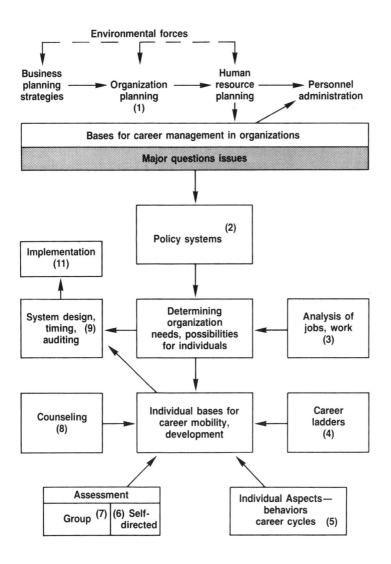

Chapter Eleven

Major Questions in Career Management

MAJOR QUESTIONS IN CAREER MANAGEMENT

This chapter addresses a number of issues most often raised by career planners and other personnel officials. They concern both human resource planning in general and career management in particular.

How do you gain the support of top management?

An initial hurdle in implementing a human resource plan is to gain support from key officials and managers who must approve it. We have found it helpful initially to visualize how top management is likely to see the program. Then the presentation of the program is tailored in the terms (i.e., costs, effects) and vocabulary that they will understand. First of all, top management must be convinced of the need and urgency of the program. Second, they must understand the objectives in practical and measurable terms.

Here are some elements to consider in persuading top management.

* Carefully assemble economic and evaluative considerations.

* Identify, where possible, potential cost improvements, (e.g., absenteeism, turnover, training, hiring).

* Outline legal requirements that may be applicable as well as specific problem areas.

* Note both tangible (costs) and intangible (inconveniences, delays, disruption of business plans) effects of the program, when these can be

expected, and the impact on other organizational
activities.

   In addition, it is important to understand the
realities of organizational life.

*   Know the power structure (i.e., who needs
     convincing?).

*   Realize that some people want to keep the status
     quo.

*   Recognize the program's effect on incumbents,
     particularly as power shifts.

*   Distinguish between what's possible and what's
     desirable.

Example – Talking Top Management's Language

   A brief example suggests some of the types of
analyses that can be made which are very effective with
top management. A human resource audit (Chapter 19) and
action research indicated a serious problem area with
second-level supervision in an insurance firm. It was the
company's position that three-fourths of all candidates
for second-level positions be brought in from the outside
to assure a regular infusion of new ideas. However,
analysis of turnover patterns indicated that newly hired
people had a turnover rate of 15 percent in the first year
whereas internally promoted candidates had on the average,
a 5 percent turnover. They also learned that the
company's internal development program was doing an
excellent job of keeping people abreast of competitive
products and developments. Also the internal study
indicated that adequate numbers of qualified candidates
were available. Thus a proposal to modify HR policy and
reverse the outside/inside recruiting ratio, (i.e., to 1/4
outside and 3/4 inside) was favorably received. Study
figures indicated that a policy change should lead to a
resolution in turnover of four people per year with a cost
savings (recruiting, hiring, training costs) of some

$40,000 annually (tangible result).   In addition, the
opportunity for organization members to qualify for the
expanded promotional opportunities was likely to have a
strong, positive effect on employees (intangible results).

What are the typical problems in implementation? One
of the most common problems is the setting of unrealistic
deadlines for implementing programs.   Other typical
problems include attempting too much at one time, lack of
participation by key officials, and building a weak base
(i.e., not enough information on jobs, poor appraisal
systems).

What establishes the common ground so that an
organization and an individual are committed to career
planning? While it is common to consider a one- to three-
year period, time span is governed by several factors:

*   the extent of organization commitment -- whether
     a specific job is being planned for or if the
     career pathing is for general career planning,

*   the level of responsibility of the individual
     involved,

*   the time needed to prepare the person,

*   the clarity of the individual's plans, and

*   the scope of uncertainties in the external
     environment.

What are some of the new methods for forecasting
long-term human resource needs for career management?
Advances in planning models and computer technology have
opened up new ways to judge future staffing requirements
(demand) and project the availability of future work force
(supply).
Forecasting external demand emphasizes exploring
alternatives, identifying likely ranges of future
activity, and developing contingency approaches. Various
mathematical and statistical models can assist in
forecasting general business demand in terms of units of

==

sales, service, or the like. These general business
requirements are then translated into personnel -- human
resource needs. Conversions are carried out on the basis,
for example, of ratios of sales to human resources with
adjustments for productivity and technological
improvements.

In the area of supply forecasting, numerous models
have been used including two that have proven quite
helpful for internal work force analyses. RENEWAL MODELS
are useful in analyzing assumptions about personnel
movement patterns. This approach considers the number of
people to be replaced (or added) at particular points in
the organization structure, and overtime. This analysis
also provides an understanding of the "ripple effect" of
certain replacement decisions in that it helps to quantify
the effects of a given personnel change in one area on
other areas of the organization. MARKOV MODELS have been
developed to deal with personnel movements over time.
They use probability tables to analyze movement flows and
the mobility of people in particular areas. For example,
they have been used to determine future replacement
(recruiting) requirements, given a particular movement
pattern (recruiting, promotions, transfers, and exits).

Does job posting work? Many job-posting systems have
successfully circulated information on job availability
and improved the identification of eligible people for
openings. Job posting has been used for a wide range of
positions including corporate officers. Information
provided by the system must be timely as well as credible
to members of the internal labor market. Job posting can
stimulate individuals to become more responsible for their
own growth opportunities. Policy areas to consider in
developing job-posting systems should include scope (jobs
and units), eligibility rules, media used, timing, format
of announcements, application forms, legitimacy of job
openings, and feedback. A well designed system also
interfaces with other personnel procedures. And, most
important, job posting relies heavily on the cooperation
of line managers for its success.

What about back-up people for succession planning?
Succession planning was among the first human resource

(manpower) programs to be established -- and then to be incorporated within the newer HRP approaches. TALENT-POOLS are increasingly being used instead of the designation of particular people, however. This makes management's choice more flexible and helps develop a broader base of talented people.

Are skill banks really useful? The system and job technology that goes into skill banks has been used in a variety of applications from helping people find jobs to establishing skill profiles for special assignments. Skill banks are effective so long as basic rules are not violated.

1. Specified skills must be demonstrated by successful job performance.

2. Selection codes must be available to show high-priority needs in the organization.

3. Information must be accessible but confined to those authorized to use it.

4. Information privacy must be safeguarded.

5. Provisions for validating and updating skill banks must exist.

6. Periodic audits are necessary for confirming continuing need accuracy and future directions.

Are there career approaches for dealing with the obsolescence of managerial and technical personnel? Obsolescence poses serious problems for managerial and technical personnel. It is commonly understood as a gap between current abilities and the requirements for the current or anticipated future job. These gaps can be caused by the phasing out of an occupation due to technical changes that outdate existing skills. They may also be due to rapid changes in product, work, or managerial technology. Career strategies have moved toward strengthening early-warning systems and improving the ability of individuals to cope with change.

==

How do we deal with the topped-out employee? The
problems of the "topped-out" employee resemble those of
obsolescence. As such, programs that deal with
obsolescence can go far in reducing topped-out employees.
Often, though, the problem is related to a range of
motivational issues, such as general job dissatisfaction,
an inability to move ahead, dull jobs, or personal
matters. The extent of company support of an individual
is also a factor to consider.

Are tuition programs obligation or strategy? Tuition
reimbursement has become a line item on the budget for
many companies. Increasingly, companies favor an approach
that ties together the career interests of individuals
with the organization's HRP requirements. This means
reviewing the degree to which individual educational
efforts help to achieve future organizational needs.

Is there an oversupply of MBAs? The demand for
graduates with advanced business training in the 1960's
and 1970's made the MBA an attractive degree. Today,
however, people with MBAs are finding it increasingly
difficult to achieve their first, or even second, job
choice. Some employers feel that they are over-qualified.
Others have taken advantage of the abundance of MBAs to
upgrade job credentials, without changing the job itself.
At the present time, much of the initial demand for MBAs
has been filled, and future requirements will proceed at a
relatively slow pace.

How do we deal with personnel problems in stagnant
organizations? In organizations that are no longer
growing, personnel is reduced to maintenance activities.
That is, a cadre of competent people usually provides
expertise and their interest is maintained through
compensation strategies or job rotation.

Is career planning practical for the small company?
While CMO can be as useful to small companies as to large
ones, there are some important differences.

     1.   There is less need for formality.

===

2.   A small company has fewer critical positions to
     keep track of.

3.   There is less sophistication in terms of
     computerized information systems.

4.   Sometimes there are greater problems with
     backing up key positions. Small companies with
     limited resources might consider using a
     consulting firm to institute a career program.

Are assessment centers practical for small companies?
A major consideration for the small company is the cost of
assessment centers. Some center procedures can be
accomplished in a day and a half and thus provide
significant benefits to offset the costs.

Can line managers be effective counselors? Most
counseling is carried out by line managers. But managers
need some training in skills such as effective listening
that were explained in Chapter 8. Two advantages spring
from using line managers as counselors:

*   The leadership aspects of the supervisor's role
     are strengthened as they demonstrate added
     capabilities.

*   Once line managers are integrated into career
     planning through counseling, their resistance to
     career programs in general is eroded.

**What are some planning problems that might arise in a
CP program?** Neglect of the planning process itself can
result in serious problems in a career program. Some
planning problems include:

*   vague or poorly developed business plans.

*   vague assumptions underlying a program or
     approach.

*   failure to establish the personnel systems upon
     which CP is based.

==

*   personnel officers taking over line managers'
        responsibilities, thereby threatening their
        authority and relations with subordinates.

*   lack of proper communication.

*   lack of credibility with officials, managers, or
        even employees, and

*   failure to train people properly to install a CP
        system.

What would be a typical time schedule for the
installation of a career program? No "typical" time
exists. A time schedule depends on the needs of a
particular organization.

What are the new directions for human resource
planning in the future? HRP is inextricably connected to
economic, legislative, and technological changes in
society. Many developments likely to be important in the
future are already underway.

1.   HRP will continue to grow in response to
        government regulation and higher costs. Even if
        regulations are relaxed in the near future,
        employment practices will likely remain the same
        because a generation of employees has grown up
        expecting them. In addition, many more
        organizations will start implementing career
        planning. As need for HRP increases, the
        practitioners will require more education and
        training.

2.   Personnel/human resource officials will have
        more responsibility and higher status. Many
        will be raised to senior officers.

3.   There will be a broadening of scope of HRP
        analyses along with a greater use of analytical
        techniques and models.

4.   Information bases will be greatly expanded.

==

5. Line management access to and use of HR
    information will increase.

6. Bases for cost-benefit determinations will be
    improved and consequently these figures will
    play a growing role in demonstrations.

7. Growing emphasis will be placed on strategic
    approaches that seek to integrate business and
    human resource and career planning.

GENERAL BIBLIOGRAPHY OF CAREER MANAGEMENT

Assessment Centers

Byham, William C. "The Assessment Center as an Aid in Management Development." Training and Development Journal 25, 12 (December 1971).

Haynes, Marion. "Streamlining an Assessment Center." Personnel Journal 55, 2 (February 1976): 80-83

Hinrichs, John and Seppo Haanpera. "Reliability of Measurement in Situational Exercises: An Assessment of Assessment Center Method." Personnel Psychology 29, 1 (January 1976): 31-40.

Huch, James and Douglas Bray. "Management Assessment Center Evaluations and Subsequent Job Performance of White and Black Females." Personnel Psychology 29, 1 (January 1976): 13-30.

Jaffee, Cabot, Joseph Bender and D. L. Calvert. "The Assessment Center Technique: A Validation Study." Management of Personnel Quarterly, 9, 3 (Fall 1970): 9-14.

Jaffee, Cabot. Interviews Conducted at Assessment Centers: A Guide for Training Managers. Dubuque, Iowa: Kendall-Hunt, 1976.

Krant, Allen I. "New Frontiers for Assessment Centers." Personnel 53, 4 (July/August 1976): 31-38.

Lupton, Daniel. "Assessing the Assessment Center: A Theory Y Approach." Personnel 50, 6 (November/ December 1973): 15-22.

==

Assessment Centers (Continued)

McConnell, John.   "The Assessment Center: A Theory Y
    Approach." Personnel 46, 2 (March/April 1969):   40-
    46.

McConnell, John and Treadway Parker.   "An Assessment
    Center Program for Multi-Organizational Use."
    Training and Development Journal 26, 3 (March 1972):
    6-14

Mitchell, James.   "Assessment Center Validity: A
    Longitudinal Study." Journal of Applied Psychology
    60, 5 (October 1975):   573-79.

Moses, Joel L. and V. R. Boehm.   "Relationships of
    Assessment Center Performance to Management Progress
    of Women." Journal of Applied Psychology 60, 4
    (1975): 528.

Moses, J. L. and William Byman, eds.   Applying the
    Assessment Center Method. New York: Pergamon Press,
    1972.

Steiner, Richard.   "New Use for Assessment Centers   --
    Training Evaluation." Personnel Journal 54, 4 (April
    1975):   236-37.

===

Career Development and General References

Albrecht, Maryann. Careers in Organizations. New York:
John Wiley and Sons, 1983.

Anderson, S. D. "Planning for Career Growth." Personnel
Journal 52, 5 (May 1973): 357-62.

Arvey, Richard D. Fairness in Selecting Employees.
Reading, MA: Addison-Wesley, 1979.

Beatty, Richard W. and Craig E. Schneier. Personnel
Administration: An Experiential Skill-Building
Approach. Reading, MA: Addison-Wesley, 1977.

Becker, G. Human Capital. New York: National Bureau of
Economic Research, 1964.

Bray, Douglas W., R. J. Campbell and D. L. Grant.
Formative Years in Business: A Long Term AT&T Study
of Managerial Lives. New York: Wiley, 1974.

Brenner, B. J. New Priorities in Training. New York:
American Management Association, 1969.

Brummet, R. Lee, Eric G. Flamholtz and William C. Pyle.
"Human Resource Accounting: A Tool to Increase
Managerial Effectiveness." Management Accounting 51,
15 (August 1969): 15.

Burack, Elmer H. and Nicholas J. Mathys. Career
Management in Organizations: A Practical Human
Resource Planning Approach. Lake Forest, IL: Brace
Park Press, 1980.

Burack, Elmer H. and Nicholas J. Mathys. Management: A
Career Oriented Approach. New York: John Wiley and
Sons, 1983.

Burack, Elmer H., Maryann Albrecht and Helen Seitler.
Growing: A Women's Guide to a Successful Career.
Belmont, CA: Lifetime Living Press, 1980.

==

Career Development and General References (Continued)

Burack, Elmer H. and Robert D. Smith. Personnel Management: A Human Resource Systems Approach. New York: John Wiley and Sons, 1982.

Byham, William C. "The Assessment Center as an Aid in Management Development." Training and Development Journal 25, 12 (December 1971)

The Career Development Bulletin, The Center for Research in Career Development, Columbia University. (Winter 1979).

Carr, Ray A. Theory and Practice of Peer Counceling. Ottawa-Hall: Canada. Occupational and Career Analyses and Development. Bunch, Canada. Employment and Immigration Comm., 1981.

Darew, Dean C. and A. J. Fredian. "Executive Career Guidance." Personnel Administration, 31, 2 (March/April 1971): 26-30.

Egan, Gerard. The Skilled Helper. Monterrey, CA: Brooks/Cole Publishing, 1975.

Ferguson, Lawrence F. "Better Management of Managers' Careers." Harvard Business Review 44, 2 (March/April 1966): 139-152.

Flamholtz, Eric. "A Model for Human Resource Valuation." The Accounting Review (April 1971).

Grusky, O. "Career Mobility and Organizational Commitment." Administrative Science Quarterly 10, 4 (March 1966): 488-503

Hall, Tim. Careers in Organizations. Pacific Palisades, CA: Goodyear Publishing Co., 1977.

Jackson, T. A. "Turned Off by Your Job?" Parts I, II, III. Industry Week 176, 5, 6, and 7 (January/February 1973).

==

Career Development and General References (Continued)

Jolson, M. A. and M. J. Gannon.   "Wives -- A Critical
    Element in Career Decisions."   Business Horizons 15,
    1 (February 1972):   83-88.

Kellog, Marian S.   Career Management   New York: American
    Management Association, 1972.

Leider, R. J. "Emphasizing Career Planning in Human
    Resource Management."   Personnel Administrator 18, 2
    (March/April 1973):   35-38.

Lippitt, Gordon L. "Developing Life Plans."   Training and
    Development Journal   24, 5 (May 1970):   2-7.

Miller, Edwin, Elmer H. Burack and Maryann Albrecht.
    Human Resource Management.   Englewood Cliffs, NJ:
    Prentice-Hall, 1980.

Moment, David and D. Fisher.   "Management Career
    Development and Confrontation."   California
    Management Review 15, 3 (Spring 1973):   46-55.

Palmer, W. J.   "An Integrated Program for Career
    Development."   Personnel Journal 51, 6 (June 1972):
    398-406.

Pinto, Patrick R., et al. Career Planning and Career
    Management: An Annotated Research Bibliography.
    Minneapolis: Industrial Relations Center, University
    of Minnesota, 1975.

Pyle, William C. "Monitoring Human Resource On-Line."
    Presentation to the National Industrial Conference
    Board.   New York City, January 20, 1970.

Roth, Laurie Michael.   A Critical Examination of the Dual
    Ladder Approach to Career Advancement.   Center for
    Research in Career Development, Columbia University,
    1982.

Career Development and General References (Continued)

Schoomaker, A. N. "Individualism in Management."
    California Management Review 11, 2 (Winter 1968): 9-
    22.

Scholz, Nelle Tumlin, Judith Sosebee Prince and Gordon
    Porter Miller. How to Decide: A Guide for Women
    New York: College Entrance Board, 1975.

Schultz, Theodore W. Investment in Human Capital. New
    York: The Free Press, 1971.

Vaughan, James A. and Samuel D. Deep. Program of
    Exercises for Management and Organizational Behavior.
    Beverly Hills, CA: Glencoe Press, 1975.

Women's Changing Roles at Home and on the Job.
    Proceedings of a Conference on the National
    Longitudinal Surveys of Mature Women in Cooperation
    with the Employed and Training Administration., U.S.
    Department of Labor. Special Reprint #26, September
    1978.

Career Patterns, Mobility Issues

Allan, P. "Career Patterns of Top Executives in New York City Government." Public Personnel Review, 33, 2 (1972): 114-117.

Astin, H. S. and A. S. Bisconti. Trends in Academic and Career Plans of College Freshmen. Bethlehem, Pennsylvania: College Placement Council, 1972.

Bailyn, Lottie and Edgar H. Schein. "Life/Career Considerations as Indicators of Quality of Employment." In A. D. Biderman and T. F. Drury (eds.), Measuring Work Quality for Social Reporting. New York: Wiley, 1976.

Basil, D. C. Woman in Management. New York: Dunnelley, 1972.

Bowin, R. B. "Middle Manager Mobility Patterns." Personnel Journal 51, 12 (1972): 878-882.

Crites, J. O. Work and Careers. In R. Dubin (ed., Handbook of Work, Organization, and Society. Chicago: Rand-McNally, 1976.

Dalton, D. R. and W. D. Todor. "Turnover Turned Over: An Expanded and Positive Perspective." Academy of Management Review 4, 2 (1979): 225-235.

Dalton, Gene. "A Review of Concepts and Research on Careers." In A. Zaleznik, G. W. Dalton, & L. B. Barnes (eds.) Orientation and Conflicts in Careers. Boston: Division of Research, Harvard Business School, 1978: 431-466.

Dalton, Gene, Paul H. Thompson, and R. Price. "Career Stages: A Model of Professional Careers in Organizations." Organizational Dynamics (Summer 1971): 19-42.

Career Patterns, Mobility Issues (Continued)

Dalton, G. W., P. H. Thompson and R. L. Price. "The Four
    Stages of Professional Careers: A New Look at
    Performance by Professionals." Organizational
    Dynamics 6 (Summer 1977): 19-42

Doeringer, P. B. "Determinants of the Structure of
    Industrial-Type Internal Labor Market". Industrial
    and Labor Relations Review 20, 2 (1967): 206-220.

Doeringer, P. G. and Michael J. Piore. Internal Labor
    Market and Manpower Analysis. Lexington,
    Massachusetts: D.C. Heath, 1971.

Driver, M. "Career Concepts and Career Management in
    Organizations." In C. L. Cooper (ed.), Behavioral
    Problems in Organizations. Englewood Cliffs, N.J.:
    Prentice-Hall, 1979.

Dyer, L. (ed.), Careers in Organizations: Individual
    Planning and Organizational Development. Ithaca,
    N.Y.: NYSSILR, Cornell University, 1976.

Edstrom, A. and Jay R. Galbraith. "Transfer of Managers
    as a Coordination and Control Strategy in
    Multinational Organizations." Administrative Science
    Quarterly 22 (1977): 248-263.

Eisenstadt, S. N. "Archetypal Patterns of Youth".
    Daedalus 91 (192): 28-46.

Elliott, C. K. "Age and Internal Labor Mobility of Semi-
    Skilled Workers." Occupational Psychology 40, 4
    (1966): 227-236

Erikson, Erik H. "Identity and the Life Cycle."
    Psychological Issues 1, 1 (1959): 1-171.

Erikson, E. H. "Identity and the Life Cycle."
    Psychological Issues 1,1 (1959): 50-100, 110-121.

Career Patterns, Mobility Issues (Continued)

Erikson, E. H., Childhood and Society. New York: Norton,
    1963.

Faulker, R. R. "Coming of Age in Organizations: A
    Comparative Study of Career Contingencies and Adult
    Socialization." Sociology of Work and Occupations 1,
    2 (1974): 131-173.

Festinger, L.   A Theory of Cognitive Dissonance.
    Evanston, IL: Row, Peterson, 1957.

Glaser, B. G. Organizational Scientists: Their
    Professional Careers. New York: Bobbs-Merrill, 1964.

Glaser, B. G. (ed.), Organizational Careers: A Source
    Book for Theory. Chicago: Aldine, 1968

Grimm, J. W. and R. N. Stern.   "Sex Roles and Internal
    Labor Market Structures: The 'Female' Semi-
    Professional." Social Problems 21, 5 (1974): 690-
    705.

Hall, D. T. and R. Mansfield.   "Relationships of Age and
    Seniority with Career Variables of Engineers and
    Scientists." Journal of Applied Psychology 60
    (1975): 201-210.

Hall, F. S. and D. T. Hall.   The Two Career Couple.
    Reading, Massachusetts: Addison-Wesley, 1979.

Harlow, D. "Professional Employees' Preference for Upward
    Mobility." Journal of Applied Psychology 57, 2
    (1973): 137-141.

Holland, J. L. The Psychology of Vocational Choice.
    Waltham, Massachusetts: Blaisdell, 1966.

Holland, John L. "Vocational Preferences."   In M. D.
    Dunnette (ed.), Handbook of Industrial and
    Organizational Psychology. Chicago: Rand-McNally,
    1976.

Career Patterns, Mobility Issues (Continued)

Katzell, R. R., R. Ewen and A. Korman. Job Attitudes of Workers from Different Ethnic Backgrounds. A Report for the U.S. Department of Labor, 1970.
Kelman, H. C. "Attitudes are Alive and Well and Gainfully Employed in the Sphere of Action. American Psychologist 29, 5 (May 1974): 310-324.

Kotter, J. P., V. A. Faux and C. McArthur. Self-Assessment and Career Development. Englewood Cliffs, N. J.: Prentice-Hall, 1978.

Knowles, M. S. The Adult Learner: A Neglected Species. Houston, Texas: Gulf Pub., 1973.

Levinson, H. "The Mid-Life Transition." Psychiatry 40 (1977): 99-112.

Louis, M. R. "Surprise and Sense Making: What Newcomers Experience in Entering Unfamiliar Organizational Settings." Administrative Science Quarterly 25, 2 (1980): 226-251.

Mahoney, Thomas A. and George T. Milkovich. "The Internal Labor Market as a Stochastic Process." In D. J. Bartholomew and A. R. Smith (eds.) Manpower and Management Science. Lexington, Massachusetts: D. C. Heath, 1971.

March, James C. and J. G. March. "Almost Random Careers: the Wisconsin School Superintendency, 1940-1972." Administrative Science Quarterly 22 (1977): 377-409.

McClelland, W. G. "Career Patterns and Organizational Needs." Journal of Management Studies 4 (1967): 56-70.

===

Career Patterns, Mobility Issues (Continued)

Milkovich, G. T., J. C. Anderson and L. Greenhalgh.
    "Organizational Careers: Environmental,
    Organizational, and Individual Determinants." in L.
    Dyer (ed.), Careers in Organizations: Individual
    Planning and Organizational Development. Ithaca:
    NYSSILR, Cornell University, 1976.

Rapoport, R. and R. N. Rapoport. Working Couples. New
    York: Harper, 1978.

Roe, A. The Psychology of Occupations. New York: Wiley,
    1956.

Rothman, R. and R. Perruci. "Organizational Careers and
    Professional Expertise." Administrative Science
    Quarterly 15, 3 (1970): 282-293.

Rotter, J. B. "Generalized Expectancies for Internal
    Versus External Control of Reinforcement."
    Psychological Monographs 80, 1 (Whole N. 609),
    (1966).

Rosebaum, J. E. "Tournament Mobility: Career Patterns in
    a Corporation." Administrative Science Quarterly 24,
    2 (1979): 220-241.

Schein, Edgar H. "The Individual, the Organization, and
    the Career: A Conceptual Scheme." Journal of
    Applied Behavioral Science 7 (1971): 401-426.

Schein, Edgar H. Career Dynamics: Matching Individual
    and Organizational Needs. Reading, MA: Addison-
    Wesley, 1978.

Schein, Edgar H. "Career Anchors and Career Paths: A
    Panel Study of Management School Graduates." In
    J. Van Maanen (ed.), Organizational Careers: Some
    New Perspectives. New York: Wiley, 1977, 49-64.

Sofer, C. Men in Mid-Career. London: Cambridge
    University Press, 1970.

Career Patterns, Mobility Issues (Continued)

Super, Donald E. The Psychology of Careers. New York:
    Harper and Row, 1957.

Super, Donald E. and Douglas T. Hall. "Career
    Development: Explorations and Planning." Annual
    Review of Psychology 29 (1978): 233-372.

Tausky, C. and Robert Dubin. "Career Anchorage:
    Managerial Mobility Motivations." American
    Sociological Review 30 (1965): 725-735.

Thompson, James D., W. R. Avery and R. O. Carison.
    "Occupations, Resources, and Careers." Education
    Administration Quarterly 4 (1968): 6-31.

Van Maanen, John. Organizational Careers: Some New
    Perspectives. New York: Wiley, 1977.

Vardi, Yoav and T. H. Hammer. "Intraorganizational
    Mobility and Career Perceptions Among Rank and File
    Employees in Different Technologies." Academy of
    Management Journal 20 (1977): 624-635.

Vroom, Victor H. Work and Motivation. New York: Wiley,
    1964.

White, H. C. "Control and Evolution of Aggregate
    Personnel: Flows of Men and Jobs." Administrative
    Science Quarterly 14, 1 (1969): 4-11.

Wilensky, H. L. "Work, Careers, and Social Integration."
    International Social Science Journal 12 (1960): 543-
    560.

Yankelovich, Daniel. "The Meaning of Work." In J. M.
    Roscow (ed.), The Worker and the Job: Coping with
    Change. Englewood Cliffs, N. J.: Prentice-Hall,
    1974.

Human Resource Information Systems[*]

Anderson, George, III. "Developing a Self Supporting Personnel Data System." The Magazine of Bank Administration 53 (February 1977): 47-50.

Burack, Elmer H. and Thomas G. Gutteridge. "Institutional Manpower Planning -- Rhetoric Versus Reality." California Management Review 20 (Spring 1978): 13-22.

Burack, Elmer H. and Nicholas J. Mathys. Chapter 8: "Human Resource Information Systems," Human Resource Planning: A Pragmatic Approach to Manpower Staffing and Development. Lake Forest, IL: Brace Park Press, 1980.

Ceriello, Vincent R. "Prepare or Defend." Journal of Systems Management 30 (April 1979): 28-30.

Ceriello, Vincent R. "A Guide for Building a Human Resource Data System." Personnel Journal 57 (1978): 496-503.

Cheek, Logan M. "Personnel Computer Systems." Business Horizons 14 (August 1971): 69.

Dukes, Carlton W. "Use of Graphic Techniques in Human Resource Management." The Personnel Administrator 21 (February 1976): 20-23.

Henderson, John C. and Paul C. Nutt. "On the Design of Planning Information Systems." Academy of Management Review 3 (1978): 774-785.

Kon, Pamela Lubin. "Automated Personnel Systems Give Billion-Dollar Banks Edge on Human Resource Management." Bank Systems and Equipment 16 (October 1978): 50-54.

Lobel, Jerome. "Privacy of Employment and Personnel Information Systems." Internal Auditor 34 (October 1977): 51-56.

==

Human Resource Information Systems (Continued)

Paretta, Robert L. "The Computer Acquisition Decision." The Personnel Administrator 23 (October 1978): 29-31.

Pfeilmeier, Frank. "Time-Sharing and Information Systems." Personnel Journal 57 (1978): 68-75.

Ratner, Stanley and Louis Leonards. "HRA On-Line Time and Attendance System." Personnel Journal 54 (August 1975: 454-455.

Robey, Daniel. "User Attitudes and Management Information Systems Use." Academy of Management Journal 22 (1979): 527-538.

Seamans, Lyman H., Jr. and Alfred J. Walker. "Questions and Answers About Employee Information Systems." Personnel Administrator 22 (November 1977): 44-49.

Shemetulskis, Richard P. "Implementing a Personnel Data System." The Personnel Administrator 23 (October 1978): 24-27.

Simonetti, J. L. and Frank Simonetti, et al. "Legal Limits in Personnel Systems." Journal of Systems Management 27 (August 1976): 34-35.

Smith, Robert D. "Information Systems for More Effective Use of Executive Resources." Personnel Journal 48 (1969): 452-465.

Smith, Robert D. "The Design and Implementation of Human Resource Information Systems." Edwin L. Miller, Elmer H. Burack, and Maryann H. Albrecht (eds.), Management of Human Resources, Englewood Cliffs, NJ: Prentice-Hall, Inc., 1980.

Southwick, Sarah and D. Diane Hatch. "Using Creative Caution in Data Base Management." The Personnel Administrator 23 (October 1978): 19-23.

Human Resource Information Systems (Continued)

Thomsen, David J. "Keeping Track of Managers in a Large
    Corporation." Personnel 53 (November/December 1976):
    23-30.

Walker, Alfred J. "Personnel Uses the Computer."
    Personnel Journal 51 (1972): 204-207.

Wilkens, Paul L. "Improving Organizational Efficiency
    Through the Dissemination of Human Resource
    Information." Academy of Management, Management
    Proceedings (August 19-22, 1973): 463-468.

---

*Compiled by Professor JoAnn Verdin, University of
Illinois At Chicago.

Human Resource Models for EEO Analysis

Atwater, D. M., Richard J. Niehaus, and J. A. Sheridan. "External Labor Market Analysis and EEO Goals Planning." U.S. Navy Office of Civilian Personnel Report 33 (April 1978).

Burroughs, J. A., S. Korn, K. A. Lewis and R. J. Niehaus. "Demographic and Upward Mobility Considerations in Using an Equal Employment Opportunity Model." U.S. Navy Office of Civilian Personnel Report 29 (October 1976).

Burroughs, J. A. and Richard J. Niehaus. "An Application of a Model and a Control System to Equal Employment Opportunity Planning." U.S. Navy Office of Civilian Personnel Report 26 (1976) and in Office of Civilian Personnel-Navy Advisor 10, 4 (Winter 1976).

Clark, Harry L. and Donna R. Thurston. Planning Your Staffing Needs: A Handbook for Personnel Workers, U.S. Civil Service Commission, Bureau of Policies and Standards, 1977, 360 pp. (Order from Superintendent of Documents, Government Printing Office, Washington, D. C. 20402, stock no. 006-000-01020-2, $5.25.)

Flast, R. H. "Taking the Guesswork out of Affirmative Action Planning." Personnel Journal 56, 2 (February 1977): 68-71. Errata, 56, 3 (March 1977): 114.

Grauer, Robert T. "An Automated Approach to Affirmative Action." Personnel 53, 5 (September/October 1976): 37-44.

Hawkins, Michael D. "Mathematical Models for Affirmative Action Goal Setting and Planning," a paper presented at the Human Resources Planning Society Conference, Atlanta, GA, March 8-10, 1978. (Available from author at Department of Management and Organization DJ-10, University of Washington, Seattle, WA 98195.)

==

Human Resource Models for EEO Analysis (Continued)

Kahalas, Harvey and David A. Gray. "A Quantitative Model
    for Manpower Decision Making." OMEGA, 4, 6 (1976):
    685-697.

Hayes, Harold. Getting the Most from EEO. New York:
    John Wiley and Sons, 1980.

Ledvinka, James. "Technical Implications of Equal
    Employment Law for Manpower Planning." Personnel
    Psychology 28 (1975): 299-323.

Snider, P. J., J. T. Royer and F. J. Baytos. Human
    Resources Planning - A Guide to Data, Equal
    Employment Advisory Council, 1747, Pennsylvania Ave.,
    N.W.,Washington D. C. 20006, $16.

"Uniform Guidelines on Employee Selection Procedures
    (1978). Adoption of Employee Selection Procedures."
    Federal Register 43, 166, Part IV (August 25, 1978):
    38290-38315.

==

Organization Commitment and Expectations

Buchanan, B. "Building Organizational Commitment: The Socialization of Managers in Work Organizations." Administrative Science Quarterly 19 (1974): 533-546.

Grusky, O. "Career Mobility and Organizational Commitment." Administrative Science Quarterly 10 (1966): 488-503.

Hall, D. T. and B. Schneider. "Correlates of Organizational Identification as a Function of Career Pattern and Organizational Type." "Administrative Science Quarterly 17 (1972): 340-350.

Hrebiniak, Lawrence C. and Joseph A. Alutto. "Personal and Role Related Factors in the Development of Organizational Commitment." Administrative Science Quarterly 17 (1972): 555-572.

Ilgen, D. W. and W. Seely. "Realistic Expectations as an Aid in Reducing Voluntary Resignations." Journal of Applied Psychology 59 (1974): 452-455.

Moore, M., E. Miller and J. Fossum. "Predictors of Managerial Career Expectations." Journal of Applied Psychology 51, 1 (1974): 90-92.

Mowday, Richard T., Richard M. Steers and Lyman W. Porter. "The Measurement of Commitment." Journal of Vocational Behavior 14 (1979): 224-247.

Reilly, R. R., S. M. Sterling and M. L. Tenopyr. "The Effects of Job Previews on Job Acceptance and Survival of Telephone Operator Candidates." Journal of Applied Psychology 64 (1979): 157-165.

Van Maanen, John. "Breaking In: Socialization to Work." In Dubin, R. (ed.), Handbook of Work, Organization and Society. Chicago: Rand-McNally, (1976, b): 67-130.

Organization Commitment and Expectations (Continued)

Wanous, John P. "Effects of a Realistic Job Preview on Job
    Acceptance, Job Attitudes, and Job Survival."
    Journal of Applied Psychology 58 (1973): 327-332.

Wanous, John P. "Organizational Entry: From Naive
    Expectations to Realistic Beliefs." Journal of
    Applied Psychology 61 (1976): 22-29.

Wanous, J. P. "Organizational Entry: Newcomers Moving
    from Outside to Inside." Psychological Bulletin 84
    (1977): 601-613.

Wanous, John P. "Organizational Entry: Recruitment,
    Selection and Socialization of Newcomers." Reading,
    MA: Addison-Wesley, 1980.

Weiner, Y. and A. S. Gechman. "Commitment: A Behavioral
    Approach to Job Involvement." Journal of Vocational
    Behavior 10 (1977): 47-52.